Critical Reasoning

A practical introduction

■ Anne Thomson

ROUTLEDGE

First published in 1996
by Routledge
11 New Fetter Lane, London EC4P 4EE

Simultaneously published in the USA and Canada
by Routledge
29 West 35th Street, New York, NY 10001

Reprinted 1998

Typeset in Sabon and Univers by
Keystroke, Jacaranda Lodge, Wolverhampton
Printed and bound in Great Britain by
TJ International Ltd, Padstow Cornwall

British Library Cataloguing in Publication Data
A catalogue record for this book is available from the British Library

Library of Congress Cataloguing in Publication Data
A catalog record for this book has been requested

ISBN 0-415-13204-5 (hbk)
ISBN 0-415-13205-3 (pbk)

Critical Reasoning

'An outstanding guide for practice at analysing arguments . . . Behind the simplicity and directness of the presentation, I sense a real mastery of the problem of how to get at the essential features of an argument'

James Cargile, *University of Virginia*

Critical reasoning focuses on giving reasons for one's beliefs and actions, on analysing and evaluating one's own and other people's reasoning, and devising and constructing better reasoning. This new and original textbook offers the opportunity to practise reasoning in a clear-headed and critical way. It will raise readers' awareness of the importance of reasoning well and help improve their skill at analysing and evaluating arguments.

Anne Thomson combines practical examples drawn from newspaper articles, such as the BSE controversy and reporting on crime statistics, with exercises designed to promote the students' ability to reason well. Her approach is valuable in four important ways:

- Practising particular skills will improve readers' ability to evaluate longer passages of reasoning.
- The use of lively topics of general interest does not require readers to have specialist knowledge.
- Model answers enable readers to check their progress throughout the book in the classroom or at home.
- A final exercise allows readers to form their own opinions on longer passages.

This stimulating new textbook encourages students to develop a range of transferable reasoning skills for any discipline, providing an invaluable foundation that will prove useful well beyond school, undergraduate or college studies.

Anne Thomson is a Fellow of the School of Economic and Social Studies at the University of East Anglia, where she lectures in philosophy. She also advises on reasoning tests for a major schools examination board.

LONDON AND NEW YORK

Contents

Acknowledgements

I am grateful to Dr Alec Fisher for his constructive comments on an earlier draft of this book, and for his suggestion of an analogy between training in sport and training in critical thinking.

Some of the ideas in this book have developed in the course of my involvement with the University of Cambridge Local Examination Syndicate's work, both on the Law Studies Test and on the MENO project. I value my involvement with colleagues on MENO, and in particular the many fruitful and stimulating discussions I have had with Dr Roy van den Brink Budgen.

Law School Admission Test questions are used with the permission of Law School Admission Council, Inc., Newtown, Pennsylvania, USA. These questions appeared on LSAT forms during the period 1981 to 1986.

I am grateful to the *Independent*, the *Guardian*, A.M. Heath and Co. (on behalf of Janet Daley), and Edwina Currie MP, for granting me permission to use articles which have been published in newspapers.

Thanks are due to my husband, Andrew, for his unfailing strong support, and to my sons, Mark and Neil. The reasoning skills of all three of them help to keep me on my toes. I should also like to thank friends involved in education who have commented on the usefulness of the approach adopted in this book – in particular Eli Cook and Pamela Homer.

Introduction

> Sir: Martin Kelly ('Fishy business in Loch Ness', 28 March) reports Dr Ian Winfield as saying that the fish stocks in Loch Ness are not big enough to feed a monster, therefore a monster does not exist. He confuses cause and effect.
>
> It is perfectly obvious to me that the reason why the fish stocks are low is because the monster keeps eating them.
>
> (*Peter Stanton, Letters to the Editor, the* Independent, *31 March 1995*)

> Sir: I read with disbelief James Barrington's letter (31 December) in which he contrasts foxhunting and fishing. He argues that the League Against Cruel Sports does not campaign against angling, because most fish which are caught are either eaten or returned to the water. Does that mean that the League would stop campaigning against foxhunting if the victims were turned into stew afterwards?
>
> (*Patricia Belton, Letters to the Editor, the* Independent, *4 January 1994*)

This is not a book about whether the Loch Ness monster exists, nor one about whether foxhunting is more cruel than angling. What the two extracts above have in common is that they are examples of reasoning – the first one perhaps tongue-in-cheek, but reasoning nevertheless. What this book

is concerned with is helping readers to develop their ability to understand and evaluate reasoning.

Reasoning is an everyday human activity. We all think about what we should do and why we should do it, and about whether – and for what reason – we should believe what other people tell us. We see examples of reasoning in our favourite soap operas on television: the single mother who allows the baby's father to help with child-minding because this will enable her to pursue her career; the parent who concludes that his daughter must be taking drugs because this is the only plausible explanation of her behaviour; and the jurors who struggle to assess whether the abused wife killed her husband owing to provocation, or in self defence, or at a time when her responsibility for her actions was diminished.

One dictionary defines reasoning as 'the act or process of drawing conclusions from facts, evidence, etc'. Since it is clear that we all do this, the purpose of this book is not to teach people to reason, but to remind them that they do not always pay attention to whether they are reasoning well, and to provide the opportunity to practise reasoning in a clear-headed and critical way. This kind of approach helps us to know whether the conclusions which are drawn from the facts or evidence really do follow, both when we ourselves are drawing conclusions and when we are assessing the reasoning of others. However, the use of the word 'critical' is not intended to suggest that when we evaluate other people's reasoning, we must restrict ourselves to saying what is wrong with it. Critical evaluation involves judging both what is good and what is bad about someone's reasoning.

Reasoning well is a skill which is valuable to anyone who wants to understand and deal with the natural and social worlds. Scientists need to reason well in order to understand the causes of phenomena. Politicians need to reason well in order to be able to adopt the right policies. But we cannot leave reasoning to scientists and politicians, because we all want to know whether what they tell us and what they prescribe for us is right. So reasoning well is an important skill for all of us.

Critical reasoning is centrally concerned with giving reasons for one's beliefs and actions, analysing and evaluating one's own and other people's reasoning, devising and constructing better reasoning. Common to these activities are certain distinct skills, for example, recognizing reasons and conclusions, recognizing unstated assumptions, drawing conclusions, appraising evidence and evaluating statements, judging whether conclusions are warranted; and underlying all of these skills is the ability to use language with clarity and discrimination.

In common with other skills, reasoning skills can be improved and polished with practice. If we think of critical reasoning as analogous to a game, we can see it as involving a set of particular skills and also the ability to deploy this set of skills when engaged in playing the game. In tennis, for example, players need to be good at executing particular strokes – driving, volleying, serving. But, in order to win a game, they need to be able to put these skills together in an appropriate way, and also be able to respond to moves made by their opponent.

When 'playing the game' of reasoning, we need to be good at certain basic activities, such as drawing conclusions and evaluating evidence. But we also need to be able to put the skills together, in order to present an effective piece of reasoning to someone else, and we need to be able to respond to the moves in reasoning made by others: for example, when someone presents us with a piece of evidence of which we were unaware, we need to be able to judge how it affects our argument. The tennis coach will improve the tennis players' ability by sometimes requiring them to practise particular skills and then to play a game in which they must remember to deploy those skills and also select the appropriate strategy.

This book offers the reader the opportunity to practise particular reasoning skills, and sometimes to 'play the game' of reasoning by deploying a set of skills. Each chapter focuses on particular skills, with short passages of reasoning on which to practise these skills. Model answers to a number of the exercises are given at the end of the book to enable readers to assess their progress. The reader's overall ability is developed by longer written passages for analysis and evaluation. As readers' command of skills improves, so their ability to analyse and evaluate the longer passages – and 'play the reasoning game' – should improve.

For the most part, these exercises offer practice in understanding, analysing and evaluating the reasoning of other people, rather than asking readers to focus on their own reasoning. There are two good reasons for this. The first is that it is necessary to illustrate the structure of reasoning, and this can only be done by presenting particular examples. The second reason is that it is often easier to recognize problems in others' reasoning than in our own. Improved skills in evaluating the reasoning of others, and the willingness to apply the same critical standards to your own reasoning, are important first steps in developing the ability to produce good reasoning of your own. Moreover, some of the exercises which suggest working with a partner, as you might do in class, will begin to make you aware of the need to present good reasons for your beliefs and conclusions, and will give you practice in responding to criticisms and questions. The final exercise suggests subjects upon which you can practise the skill of devising and constructing better reasoning of your own.

It has already been pointed out that the ability to reason well is important in everyday life – in understanding, for example, the reasons upon which politicians base their policies, or the evidence presented in a court of law. It is also true that almost every subject of academic study, both at school and at university, requires an ability to reason well. However, most subjects are not taught in a way which requires students to think about their own thinking processes. Hence it is possible to become good at reasoning about, say, geography, without realizing that you have developed skills which apply in other areas. The approach presented in this book does not require any specialist knowledge – the passages of reasoning are on topics of general interest, such as would be discussed in newspapers and can be understood by the general public. But it does require you to think about the nature of reasoning, so as to acquire the tendency to approach reasoning on any topic in this critical, analytic way. In other words, these reasoning skills are transferable; they will help students in their reasoning on a wide range of topics, including their own specialist area. Practice in dealing with reasoned argument will also help students in their essay writing, since in most subjects a requirement of good essay writing is that ideas should be presented in a clear, coherent and well argued way.

The ideas underlying this text are related to the academic discipline known as Critical Thinking, as can be seen from the following quotation from Edward Glaser, co-author of the world's most widely used test of critical thinking, the Watson–Glaser Critical Thinking Appraisal: 'Critical thinking calls for a persistent effort to examine any belief or supposed form of knowledge in the light of the evidence that supports it and the further conclusions to which it tends' (Glaser 1941; 5). This Critical Thinking tradition, which derives from both philosophy and education, originated in the USA. Some of its foremost American proponents were, or are, John Dewey, Edward Glaser, Steven Norris, Robert Ennis, Richard Paul and Michael Scriven; in Britain, the name most closely associated with Critical Thinking is that of Alec Fisher. Readers who are interested in learning more about the subject will find details of these authors' works in the bibliography at the end of this book.

In recent years, materials for assessing Critical Thinking have been developed by the University of Cambridge Local Examinations Syndicate, as one component of the MENO Thinking Skills Service. This service is intended for use by institutions of higher education, by employers, and by organizations concerned with professional training and vocational education, and it aims to assess students' and prospective students' potential.

However, the skills of critical reasoning are valuable not simply in an educational context. Once developed, they should enable readers to deal effectively with reasoning in every sphere of their lives.

Chapter 1

Analysing reasoning

We cannot begin to evaluate someone's reasoning if we do not understand it, or if we understand the words but fail to grasp that reasons are being offered for accepting a point of view. The skills upon which this chapter focuses – recognizing reasoning, and identifying conclusions, reasons and assumptions – are the most basic abilities; upon them the important skills involved in *evaluating* reasoning (the focus of our next chapter) depend.

Recognizing reasoning and identifying conclusions

Reasoning is, of course, presented in language, but not all communications in language involve reasoning, so we need to be able to pick out those features of language which tell us that reasoning is taking place. It is clear that we use language for a variety of purposes. For example, we may use it to tell a joke, to insult someone, to report factual information, to describe a scene or a personality, to tell a story, to express our feelings, to explain why we have acted in a particular way, to ask questions, to issue orders. What most uses of language have in common is the attempt to communicate something to others.

Sometimes we want to persuade others to accept the truth of a statement, and one way of doing this is to offer them reasons or evidence in support of this statement. This is the essence of argument. The simplest examples of arguments occur when someone, who believes some statement, will present reasons which aim at persuading others to adopt this same point of view. In more complex cases, someone may wish to assess and evaluate someone else's reasoning, or someone may be reasoning about their own or someone else's reasoning. We all use language in this way, often without thinking of what we are doing as being something so grand as 'presenting an argument'. For example, someone might say:

> He must be older than he says he is. He told us he was forty-two, but he has a daughter who is at least thirty years old.

Here reasons are being offered for the conclusion that 'he must be older than he says he is'. So this simple, everyday piece of communication is an argument.

Here are some more very simple examples of argument. As you read through these examples, think about which statement the author is trying to get you to accept (that is, the conclusion) and which statements are being offered as reasons for accepting the conclusion:

> The bus is late. It must have broken down.

> That bird can't be a robin. It doesn't have a red breast.

> You should try to appear confident in your job interview. The employers are looking for someone who can speak confidently in public.

> Children learn languages much more quickly and speak them more fluently if they start to learn them at an early age. So if you want your children to be bilingual, you should speak two languages to them from the time they are born.

> She didn't turn up for their date. She obviously doesn't really want to be his girlfriend. If she'd wanted a serious relationship with him she wouldn't have missed the date.

Argument indicator words

The language of reasoning can be very complex, but there are some relatively simple linguistic clues which can signal that reasoning is taking place. Certain characteristic words are used to indicate that someone is presenting a conclusion, the most commonly used being 'therefore' and 'so'. For example, the argument presented in the first paragraph of this section could be written as:

He told us he was forty-two, but he has a daughter who is at least thirty years old. So, he must be older than he says he is.

'Hence' and 'thus' can also function in the same way as 'so' and 'therefore', though they are less commonly used. Other words may indicate the presence of a conclusion, for example, 'must', 'cannot'. In the original version above, the word 'must' is used to show that the reasons offered force us to draw the conclusion. The word 'cannot' could function in a similar way, since the conclusion could have been expressed as follows: 'He cannot be as young as he says he is'.

Sometimes the word 'should' can signal that someone is presenting a conclusion, because arguments often make a recommendation. This is shown in two of the examples above; the third, which recommends appearing confident in a job interview, and the fourth, which recommends speaking two languages to babies. All of these conclusion indicator words have other uses in addition to their function in arguments, so their presence in a written passage does not guarantee that an argument is being offered. However, they are useful indicators in assessing whether a passage contains an argument.

Recognizing arguments without argument indicator words

Some passages which contain arguments have no argument indicator words. In order to recognize them as arguments, it is necessary to consider the relationships between statements in the passage, to assess whether some of the statements can be taken to support a statement expressing a conclusion. For example, the following passage can be construed as an argument:

Knowing the dangers of smoking is not sufficient to stop people from smoking. One third of the population still smokes. Everyone must know that smoking causes lung cancer and heart disease.

This passage is clearly presenting as a statistical fact that one third of the population smokes, and as an obvious truth that everyone must know the dangers of smoking. It is using these reasons to support the conclusion that knowing the dangers is not sufficient to stop smokers from smoking.

Note that the only candidate for a conclusion indicator – the word 'must' – appears not in the conclusion, but in one of the reasons. Yet, we can be clear that the last sentence is not the conclusion, because no appropriate evidence (for example, that there have been programmes to educate the public about the dangers) is offered. Note also that in this example, as well as in our first example, the conclusion does not appear at the *end* of the passage. We need to be aware that conclusions can appear anywhere within a passage, even though it is possible for us to 'tidy up' an argument by writing out the reasons first and ending with a conclusion introduced by 'so' or 'therefore'.

We have now considered two things we might look for to identify the conclusion of an argument:

1 conclusion indicator words,
2 the claim for which reasons appear to be offered.

Note that if we have identified a conclusion, we have also identified the passage as an argument, or as something which is intended to be an argument. If we have identified the conclusion by finding conclusion indicator words, then it is reasonable to regard the author as *intending* to present an argument. Earlier, we introduced the term 'argument' as one way in which people use language when they are attempting to persuade or convince others of the truth of something – that is to say, when they have a particular purpose. However, when trying to assess whether a written passage presents an argument, we are not solely trying to guess the purpose of the author in writing the passage. We can also attempt to interpret the way in which this piece of language functions: this is what we are doing when we identify the conclusion by the second method, that is to say by looking for the claim for which reasons appear to be offered. If a passage can be written out as a series of reasons supporting a conclusion, then it can be construed as an argument, even if the author did not quite intend it in that way.

Nevertheless, it is often useful as a first step to consider the purpose of a passage when trying to decide whether it is an argument. If you ask yourself, 'What is the main point which this passage is trying to get me to accept or believe?', you can then underline the sentence which you think expresses the main point. The next step is to check whether the rest of the passage contains a reason or series of reasons which support the main point. You need not worry too much at this stage about whether they give conclusive support, because you are not yet attempting to evaluate the reasoning. Consider whether they are relevant to the main point, and whether they support it, rather than counting against it. Do they provide the kind of evidence or reasoning one would need to present in order to establish the truth of the main point? If you are satisfied on these matters, then you can take it that you have identified a conclusion of an argument, and thereby decided that the passage is an argument. You may find it useful to tidy up the argument by writing it out as a series of reasons, followed by your chosen conclusion, introduced by 'So' or 'Therefore'.

Identifying conclusions

In this section are some examples in which we put these recommendations into practice.

> The new miracle drug Amotril has caused unforeseen side effects of a devastating nature. Careful testing of the drug prior to its marketing could have prevented the problems caused by these side effects. Therefore, no new drugs should be released for public consumption without a thorough study of their side effects.
>
> (*Law School Admission Test, 1981*)

This argument presents its conclusion in a straightforward way, and this helps to make it an easy passage to analyse. We first notice that the word 'Therefore' introduces the last sentence, so it is obvious that the conclusion we are being led to accept is:

> no new drugs should be released for public consumption without a thorough study of their side effects.

The reason given for this is that careful testing of Amotril before it went on sale could have prevented the problems caused by its devastating side effects. In this case, we do not need to tidy up the argument, since it is clear what claim is being made. Moreover, the reason gives good support for the conclusion, provided we assume that one could not find out about a drug's side effects without thorough study, and that it is never worth taking the risk of offering a drug for sale unless we are as certain as we can be that it has no serious side effects.

Here is another example:

> People who diet lose weight. Pavarotti cannot have dieted. He hasn't lost weight.

In this case, we do not have a conclusion indicator such as 'So' or 'Therefore', but we do have the word 'cannot'. Is it being used to signal a conclusion? We must consider whether the sentence in which it occurs is the main point which the passage is trying to establish. It seems that the passage *is* trying to convince us that Pavarotti cannot have dieted, and we seem to have a clear argument if we rearrange it to read:

> People who diet lose weight. Pavarotti hasn't lost weight. Therefore, he cannot have dieted.

This is the most natural way to read the passage.

But suppose we had started out by assuming that the *main* point which the passage was aiming to get us to accept was that Pavarotti has not lost weight. Then, we would have set out the argument as follows:

> People who diet lose weight. Pavarotti cannot have dieted. Therefore, he hasn't lost weight.

But this is an unnatural reading of the passage, in two respects. First, it would not be natural to use the words 'cannot have dieted' in the second sentence if the meaning it aimed to convey was that Pavarotti has been unable to diet. Secondly, even if we replaced 'cannot have dieted' with 'has been unable to diet', the first two sentences would be insufficient to establish the conclusion, since Pavarotti may have lost weight by some means other than dieting, for example by taking exercise. Moreover, the kind of evidence one would have to use to establish that Pavarotti had not lost weight would be evidence, not about whether or not he had dieted, but about what he weighed in the past compared with what he weighs now.

Here is another example in which there are no conclusion indicators such as 'so' and 'therefore':

> We need to make rail travel more attractive to travellers. There are so many cars on the roads that the environment and human safety are under threat. Rail travel should be made cheaper. Everyone wants the roads to be less crowded, but they still want the convenience of being able to travel by road themselves. People will not abandon the car in favour of the train without some new incentive.

What is the main point which this piece of reasoning tries to get us to accept? Clearly it is concerned with suggesting a way of getting people to switch from using cars to using trains, on the grounds that it would be a good thing if people did make this switch. We could summarize the passage as follows:

> Because the large numbers of cars on the roads are bad for the environment and human safety, and because people will not abandon the car in favour of the train without some new incentive, we need to make rail travel more attractive. So, rail travel should be made cheaper.

Notice that the word 'should' appears in the conclusion. This may have helped you to see which sentence was the conclusion. Now that we can see more clearly what the argument is, we may question whether it is a good argument. For example, is it the *cost* of rail travel which deters motorists from switching to using trains, or is it because rail travel is less convenient? Would reducing rail fares really make a difference? Are there any alternative measures which would better achieve the desired effect? Setting out the argument in this way can help us to see what questions we need to ask when we begin to evaluate arguments.

Judging whether a passage contains an argument

Sometimes the subject matter of a passage may make it appear at first sight that an argument is being presented when it is not. Consider these two passages, one of which can be construed as an argument, whereas the other cannot.

> The number of crimes reported to the police is rising. The overall crime rate may not be rising. Traditionally, only a quarter of what most people regard as crime has been notified to the police.

> Most crime is committed by those aged under 21. But most people aged under 21 are not criminals. Some people aged over 21 are persistent offenders.

Let us consider the first passage and ask what main point it is making. Does it try to convince us that the number of crimes reported to the police is rising? It presents no evidence for this, but simply presents it as a fact. Does it try to convince us that traditionally, only a quarter of what most people regard as crime has been notified to the police? Again, no evidence is offered for this. Does it offer evidence for the claim that the overall crime rate may not be rising? Well, it gives us information which shows that this is a possibility. The fact that reported crime is rising may make us suspect that crime is rising overall. But when we are told that there has been a tendency for only a quarter of what is regarded as crime to be reported, we can see that if this tendency has changed in such a way that a greater fraction of what is perceived as crime is now reported, then the overall crime rate may not be rising after all. We can write this argument as follows:

> Traditionally, only a quarter of what most people regard as crime has been notified to the police. So, although the number of crimes reported to the police is rising, the overall crime rate may not be rising.

Notice that the original version of this passage did not contain any of the 'argument indicator' words which we have listed, but it is nevertheless an argument.

Now let us look at the second passage. What does it aim to get us to believe? It presents three comments about statistics on crime, each of which, in a sense, it aims to get us to believe, since it asserts them as being true. However, it does not have a single major point to make, in the sense that none of the statements supports any of the others. You will see this if you try for yourself writing out the three possible ways of treating one of the statements as a conclusion. So this is a passage in which three pieces of information about the same subject-matter are not linked in any process of reasoning; but, because of the kind of information presented, that is to say, because it refers to statistics, we may at first be tempted to think of it as an argument, because the use of statistics is a common move in argument. We need to be aware, then, that argument is not just a matter of presenting information – it is, rather, a matter of presenting a conclusion based on information or reasons.

Summary: Is it an argument?

Here is a summary of the steps to take when trying to assess whether a passage is an argument:

1 Look for '*conclusion indicator*' words, i.e. words such as 'so', 'therefore', 'must', 'cannot', 'should'.
2 If there are no 'conclusion indicator' words, look at each sentence in turn and ask, '*Does the rest of the passage give any extra information which tells me why I should believe this*?' If the answer is 'No', then this sentence is not a conclusion. If the answer is 'Yes', then the sentence is a conclusion.
3 If none of the sentences in a passage is a conclusion, then the passage is not an argument: *no conclusion, no argument.* If one of the sentences in a passage is a conclusion supported by a reason or reasons in the rest of the passage, then the passage is an argument.
4 When you have found a conclusion in a passage, rewrite the passage with the conclusion at the end, introduced by 'So'. Read through this re-written passage to check that it makes sense. If it does, then you can be certain that this passage is an argument.

Do not worry at this stage about whether the reasons are true, or about whether they give conclusive support to the conclusion.

Exercise 1: Identifying arguments and conclusions

For each of the following passages:

- decide whether it is an argument and
- if it is an argument say what the conclusion is.

1 Before they start school, all children need to acquire many skills, for example, speaking, dressing, washing, identifying colours. Parents should be perfectly capable of teaching these skills. Instead of spending money on nursery education, we should spend it on educating people to become good parents.

2 Human beings learn more between birth and the age of five than at any other time in their lives. Ninety per cent of three and four year olds receive

some form of pre-school education. More than fifty per cent of children aged under five attend school.

3 Red squirrels can eat yew berries, hawthorn berries and rosehips. Grey squirrels can eat none of these. However, grey squirrels eat acorns which red squirrels cannot eat.

4 Millions of pounds of public money are spent defending riverside farmland from flooding. Some of this money should be given to farmers to compensate them for taking such land out of production. This would save money and would benefit the environment, since if rivers were allowed to flood, their natural flood plains would provide wetland meadows and woodland rich in wildlife.

5 The Meteorological Office in Bracknell said total rainfall in England and Wales for the autumn months had been 34 per cent above the long-term average. December was wetter still – 57 per cent above the average for the month in England and Wales. Scotland has also had a wet autumn and winter.

6 The North American Wildlife Federation, which sponsors an annual watch for endangered species, reports that sightings of the bald eagle between 1978 and 1979 increased by 35 per cent. In the watch of 1979, 13,127 sightings of bald eagles were reported, 3,400 over the 1978 count. This indicates considerable growth in the bald eagle population.

(*Law School Admission Test, 1981*)

7 In recent years, the demand for computer-literate personnel has increased. More students are graduating in computing science than before. Some companies find that these graduates require further training before embarking on a career in computing.

8 We could reduce road accidents by lowering speed limits, and making greater efforts to ensure that such limits are enforced. But, because this would inconvenience the majority who drive safely, this would be an unacceptable solution to the problem of careless drivers who are unsafe at current speed limits.

9 Wealth should be distributed more evenly. The purpose of distributing wealth must be to produce more happiness. The same amount of wealth will yield more happiness if it is distributed widely than if it is divided with great inequality. A dollar to a poor man means more than a dollar to a rich man – in that it meets more urgent needs and, therefore, produces more happiness.

10 Government campaigns against smoking are always based on the assumption that the greatest risk to health from smoking is the risk of getting lung cancer. But this is not so. It is true that heavy smoking roughly doubles a person's chance of dying of heart disease, whereas it increases

the chance of dying from lung cancer by about ten times. But we have to take into account the fact that there is a much higher incidence of heart disease than of lung cancer in the general population. This means that for every smoker who develops lung cancer, there will be about three who die of self-induced heart disease.

Identifying reasons

We use reasons in a number of ways, for example to support conclusions of arguments, to support recommendations, to explain why something has happened or why someone has acted in a particular way. This section focuses on the use of reasons to support conclusions of arguments.

If we have identified a conclusion of an argument which has no argument indicator words, then it is likely that we will already have some idea as to what the reasons of the argument are, since in order to identify the conclusion, we will have had to assess which parts of the passage could be taken to give to support to the chosen conclusion – hence which parts are the reasons. This is what you were doing when you worked through Exercise 1. But if we identify the conclusion by the presence of argument indicator words, then we will have to look again at the passage in order to identify the reasons.

Sometimes we will find characteristic words which indicate the presence of reasons, words such as 'because', 'for', 'since'. For example, our earlier argument about Pavarotti could have read as follows:

> People who diet lose weight. Since Pavarotti hasn't lost weight, he cannot have dieted.

In this example, the word 'Since' signals that 'Pavarotti hasn't lost weight' is being offered as a reason for the conclusion that Pavarotti cannot have dieted. Sometimes a phrase will be used which tells us explicitly that a reason is being offered, a phrase such as 'the reason for this is'; and sometimes reasons are listed, introduced by the words 'firstly . . . secondly . . . [and so on]'.

Arguments often use hypothetical or conditional statements as reasons. These are statements which begin with 'If' (or 'when' or 'where') and which say that something is true, or will be true, or will happen, provided that (on the condition that) something else is true or something else occurs – for example, 'If I read without wearing my glasses, I will get a headache.' When you see a sentence beginning with the word 'If', think about whether this sentence is being offered as one of the reasons for a conclusion. It is important to remember that it is the whole statement which is being presented as a reason. You should not attempt to break the statement down into two reasons. Sometimes an argument has a hypothetical statement for a conclusion, so you cannot just assume that any hypothetical statement is being offered as a reason.

In common with conclusion indicator words, these reason indicator words can be used in ways other than to introduce a reason, so their presence cannot guarantee that a reason is being offered – but it can be a useful clue. Sometimes, however, we will find no such words or phrases, and will have to rely on our understanding of the meaning of the passage. It may be useful to ask yourself, 'What kind of reason would I have to produce in order to provide support for this conclusion?' You should then look in the passage to see if such reasons are offered.

In addition to the hypothetical statements already mentioned, many different kinds of statements can function as reasons. They may be items of common knowledge, general principles, reports of the results of experiments, statistics, and so on. What they have in common is that they are put forward as being true. Not all the reasons offered in an argument can be given support *within that argument*. That is to say, arguments have to start somewhere, so every argument must offer at least one basic reason for which no support is offered. Thus those who present arguments will often take as a starting point something which is obviously true, or the truth of which can easily be checked by others. However, this is not always the case. People may present something which is contentious as a basic reason, and they may fail to give support for such a statement precisely in order to conceal the contentious nature of their argument. So the evaluation of reasoning, which will be discussed in the next chapter, will require us to consider whether the basic reasons presented in any argument are true.

The structure of arguments

The reasons in an argument can fit together in a number of ways. Sometimes there may be only one reason supporting a conclusion, for example:

> Pavarotti is thinner. So he has probably been dieting.

In our original Pavarotti argument, there are two reasons:

> Reason 1 People who diet lose weight.
>
> Reason 2 Pavarotti hasn't lost weight.

These two reasons, *taken together*, support the conclusion:

> Pavarotti cannot have dieted.

Neither reason on its own would be sufficient to support the conclusion. The number of reasons used in this way in an argument need not be limited to two. An argument could have three, four or a whole string of reasons which need to be taken together in order to support the conclusion.

However, sometimes when there are two (or more) reasons, they are offered not as jointly supporting the conclusion, but as independently supporting it, for example:

> Cigarette advertising should be banned because it encourages young people to start smoking. But even if it had no such influence on young people, it should be banned because it gives existing smokers the mistaken impression that their habit is socially acceptable.

In this case, the conclusion that cigarette advertising should be banned could be supported either by the claim that it has the adverse effect of encouraging young people to start smoking, or by the claim that it has the adverse effect of making smokers think that their habit is socially acceptable. Unlike the Pavarotti argument, the author of this argument does not regard it as necessary to offer both reasons, and would claim that the argument had established its conclusion if *either* reason could be shown to be true. But when an argument offers reasons as jointly supporting the conclusion, then evaluating the argument requires an assessment of the truth of *all* the reasons.

In the two examples we have just presented, it is clear that in one case joint reasons, and in the other case independent reasons, are being offered. But in some arguments it will be debatable whether the reasons are intended to support the conclusion jointly or independently. Consider the following example:

> Our 40,000 GIs stationed in South Korea support a corrupt regime. The savings in dollars which would result from their coming home could make a sizable dent in the projected federal deficit. Furthermore, the Korean conflict ended 30 years ago. Hence it is time we brought our troops home.
>
> (*James B. Freeman, Thinking Logically, p. 165*)

In this case each one of the first three sentences presents a reason for the conclusion, which appears in the last sentence. Because they are all quite strong reasons for the claim that the troops should be brought home, it may be that the author regards them as independently supporting the conclusion. On the other hand, if they are taken jointly, they present a much stronger case for the conclusion. We could interpret the argument either way here, but it should be remembered in cases like this that, provided all the reasons are true, the argument could be judged to be stronger if it is interpreted as presenting joint rather than independent reasons.

Arguments can become much more complicated than the above examples. Reasons may be offered for a conclusion which is then used, either on its own or together with one or more other reasons, in order to draw a further conclusion. It is useful to make a distinction in such cases between an *intermediate conclusion* and a *main conclusion*. Here is an example of an argument with an intermediate conclusion.

> A majority of prospective parents would prefer to have sons rather than daughters. So, if people can choose the sex of their child, it is likely that eventually there will be many more males than females in the population. A preponderance of males in the population is likely to produce serious social problems. Therefore, we should discourage the use of techniques which enable people to choose the sex of their child.

The main conclusion here, signalled by 'Therefore', is that

> we should discourage the use of techniques which enable people to choose the sex of their child.

The immediate reasons given (jointly) for this are:

> if people can choose the sex of their child, it is likely that eventually there will be many more males than females in the population

and:

> A preponderance of males in the population is likely to produce serious social problems.

The first of these two reasons is itself a conclusion, signalled by the word 'So', which follows from the basic reason that

> A majority of prospective parents would prefer to have sons rather than daughters.

Thus an analysis of this passage reveals that the first sentence is a *basic reason*, which supports the *intermediate conclusion* expressed in the second sentence, which in turn, taken jointly with the additional reason offered in the third sentence, supports the *main conclusion* in the last sentence. Unfortunately, not all arguments will set out their reasons and conclusions in this obvious order of progression, so you cannot simply take it for granted that basic reasons will always appear at the beginning, with intermediate conclusions in the middle and main conclusion at the end.

We have identified two important approaches to identifying the reasons which are being offered in an argument – first, asking what kind of reason could give support to a particular conclusion, and secondly, attempting to sort out the way in which the reasons in a passage hang together. It may seem that detailed knowledge of the subject matter will be necessary before one can begin to analyse the argument, and no doubt it is true that the more familiar you are with the subject matter, the more readily will you be able to work out the structure of the argument. However, on many topics, most people will be able to go a long way towards understanding arguments which they encounter in newspapers and textbooks, and they will improve at this task with the kind of practice afforded by the following sets of exercises.

Exercise 2: Offering reasons for conclusions

Working with a partner, take it in turns to think of a simple claim which you think you have good reason to believe. (For example, you may think that there should be speed limits lower than 30 mph on housing estates, because cars travelling at 30 mph on streets where children play can easily cause road deaths.) Tell your partner what your 'conclusion' is (in this example 'Speed limits on housing estates should be lower than 30 mph'). Your partner must then try to offer a reason for this. They may not come up with your reason, but they may come up with another good reason. What you are practising in this exercise is thinking about the *relevance* and the *strength* of potential reasons. You may not come up with the strongest reason, but you should aim to produce something which is clearly relevant, and gives some support to the conclusion, rather than being neutral or counting against it.

Exercise 3: Identifying reasons

This exercise also gives you practice in assessing what could count as a reason for a given 'conclusion'. In each question, pick the answer which could be a reason for accepting the truth of the conclusion, and say why this is the right answer, and why the other options are wrong. Note that you are not to worry about whether the reason is true. You must just consider whether, if it were true, your chosen reason would support the conclusion.

1 Conclusion: Blood donors should be paid for giving blood.

(a) The Blood Donor service is expensive to administer.
(b) People who give blood usually do so because they want to help others.
(c) There is a shortage of blood donors, and payment would encourage more people to become donors.

2 Conclusion: When choosing someone for a job, employers should base their decision on the applicants' personalities, rather than on their skills.

(a) Personalities may change over time, and skills go out of date.
(b) Skills can easily be taught, but personalities are difficult to change.
(c) Some skills cannot be acquired by everyone, but everyone can develop a good personality.

3 Conclusion: Light-skinned people should avoid exposure to the sun.

(a) Ultra-violet light from the sun can cause skin cancer on light skins.
(b) Dark-skinned people do not suffer as a result of exposure to the sun.
(c) Light-skinned people can use sun creams in order to avoid sunburn.

4 Conclusion: Installing insulation in your house may be economical in the long run.

(a) Less fuel is needed to heat a house which has been insulated.
(b) In a house which has been insulated the air feels warmer.
(c) Some types of insulation cause houses to be damp.

5 Conclusion: In order to reduce crime, we should not use imprisonment as a punishment for young offenders.

(a) Young offenders could be taught job skills whilst in prison.
(b) It would be expensive to build new prisons to relieve prison over-crowding.
(c) Young offenders are more likely to re-offend if their punishment has been a term of imprisonment.

6 Conclusion: Sam could not have committed the murder.

(a) Sally had both the opportunity and a motive to commit the murder.
(b) Sam could not have gained anything by committing the murder.
(c) Sam was several miles away from the scene of the murder when the victim was stabbed to death.

7 Conclusion: A vegetarian diet may be beneficial to health.

(a) A vegetarian diet lacks certain important vitamins.
(b) A vegetarian diet excludes animal fats which can cause heart disease.
(c) A vegetarian diet excludes fish oil which is thought to be beneficial to health.

8 Conclusion: Parents should be strongly recommended to have their children vaccinated against polio.

(a) Some parents think that there is a risk of harmful side effects from the polio vaccine.
(b) If a substantial percentage of the population is not vaccinated against polio, there will be outbreaks of the disease every few years.
(c) The risk of becoming infected with polio is very low.

9 Conclusion: Those people who die from drowning are more likely to be swimmers than to be non-swimmers.

(a) People who cannot swim are much more likely than swimmers to avoid risky water sports.
(b) Many deaths from drowning occur because people on boating holidays fail to wear life-jackets.

(c) Even those who can swim may panic if they fall into the sea or a river.

10 Conclusion: Some types of chewing-gum are bad for the teeth.

(a) Some chewing-gums are sweetened with sorbitol, which helps to neutralize tooth-rotting acids.
(b) The action of chewing gum can get rid of particles of sugar trapped between the teeth.
(c) Some chewing-gums are sweetened with sugar, which causes tooth decay.

Answers to Exercise 3 are given on p. 123.

Exercise 4: Identifying parts of an argument

For each of the following arguments, identify the main conclusion and the reasons. Say whether there are any intermediate conclusions. Say whether the reasons support the conclusion jointly or independently.

1 The odds that a dangerous leak from a nuclear power plant could occur are so small as to be almost impossible to calculate. I have as much chance of being seriously injured backing out of my drive as I would living next to a nuclear power plant for a year. So someone living next door to a nuclear power plant should feel 100 per cent safe.

2 The one third of people who smoke in public places are subjecting the rest of us to discomfort. What is more, they are putting our health at risk, because 'passive' smoking causes cancer. That is why it is time to ban smoking in public places.

3 The existence of God is not self-evident to us. Yet from every effect the existence of the cause can be clearly demonstrated, and so we can demonstrate the existence of God from His effects. Hence the existence of God, insofar as it is not self-evident to us, can be demonstrated from those of His effects which are known to us.

4 Radioactive elements disintegrate and eventually turn into lead. So if matter has always existed there should be no radioactive elements left. The presence of uranium and other radioactive elements is scientific proof that matter has not always existed.

5 A foetus's heart is beating by 25 days after fertilization. Abortions are typically done seven to ten weeks after fertilization. Even if there were any doubt about the fact that the life of each individual begins at fertilization, abortion clearly destroys a living human being with a beating heart and a functioning brain. If the first right of a human being is the right to his or

her life, the direct killing of an unborn child is a manifest violation of that right.

6 It has always been the case in the past that new discoveries of mineral reserves have kept pace with demand. For example, bauxite reserves have tripled in the last ten years, while demand has doubled over the same period. At no time have the known reserves of minerals been as great as the total mineral resources of the world. Therefore, even though at any given time we know of only a limited supply of any mineral, there is no reason for us to be concerned about running out of mineral resources.

7 In rape cases, sentences should be lighter for those who plead guilty than for those who plead not guilty. For a victim of rape, appearing in court is a very distressing experience. If the defendant pleads guilty, the victim does not have to appear in court. If sentences are as heavy for those who plead guilty as for those who plead not guilty, all defendants will plead not guilty, because there is nothing to lose.

8 If imprisonment worked as a deterrent to potential criminals, the more people we had in prison to serve as examples, the more would their lesson be conveyed to those outside prison. But today we have record numbers of people in prison, and a crime rate which is growing, not decreasing. Thus, imprisonment is not an effective deterrent.

9 Those who oppose any and all restrictions on freedom of the press are wrong. Consider the effects of freedom to report on cases of kidnap. Experience shows that kidnap victims are less likely to be killed by their captors if the kidnapping is not reported. To report a kidnap can thus endanger a victim's life. If we do not pass legislation against publishing in these circumstances, some newspapers will continue to be irresponsible and will publish details of the kidnapping before the victim is released or rescued.

10 [If killing an animal infringes its rights, then] never may we destroy, for our convenience, some of a litter of puppies, or open a score of oysters when nineteen would have sufficed, or light a candle in a summer evening for mere pleasure, lest some hapless moth should rush to an untimely end. Nay, we must not even take a walk, with the certainty of crushing many an insect in our path, unless for really important business! Surely all this is childish. In the absolute hopelessness of drawing a line anywhere, I conclude that man has an absolute right to inflict death on animals, without assigning any reason, provided that it be a painless death, but that any infliction of pain needs its special justification.

(Lewis Carroll, 'Some popular fallacies about vivisection', in The Complete Works of Lewis Carroll, Nonesuch, 1939, p. 1072)

Answers to Exercise 4 are given on p. 126.

Exercise 5: Thinking about assumptions

Here is a slightly longer passage of reasoning taken from an article in a newspaper, discussing whether Bill Clinton, the President of the USA, should be criticized for his alleged sexual involvements with women other than his wife. The following points may make it easier to understand the passage:

- The author uses the word 'syllogism' in the second sentence, but it is used inaccurately. A syllogism is a particular form of argument. What the author describes as a syllogism is simply a hypothetical statement.
- In the first paragraph the author refers to Richard Nixon, a former president of the United States, and says that 'the American people could not be sure where he was during the day'. This is a reference to the widespread perception of Nixon as being an untrustworthy politician. His nickname was 'Tricky Dickie'.

Now read the passage, say what you think is its main conclusion, and write down a list of assumptions which you think it makes.

> Two justifications are generally given for the examination of a politician's sex life. The first is the prissy syllogism that 'if a man would cheat on his wife, he would cheat on his country'. But Gerry Ford and Jimmy Carter were, by most accounts, strong husbands but weak presidents. I would guess that Pat Nixon knew where Dick was every night. The problem was that the American people could not be sure where he was during the day. Conversely, it is a sad but obvious fact that, to many of those men to whom he gave unusual political nous, God handed out too much testosterone as well.
>
> The second excuse for prurience towards rulers is that leaders, tacitly or explicitly, set examples to the nation and thus their own slips from grace are hypocritical. But Bill Clinton, unlike many senior US politicians, has never publicly claimed that he has led an entirely decent life.
>
> And if the United States does wish to impose strict standards of sexual morality on its leaders, then it must properly address the Kennedy paradox. A month ago in Dallas, I watched people weep and cross themselves at the minute of the 30th anniversary of JFK's assassination. If only he had lived, they said then, and millions of middle-aged Americans say it daily. They construct a cult of stolen greatness. But if JFK had lived, he would have been trashed weekly by bimbo anecdotes in the supermarket magazines. If he had run for President in the Eighties, he wouldn't have got beyond New Hampshire before the first high-heel fell on television.
>
> So we must tell the snipers not to fire at Bill Clinton [because of his sex life].
>
> (*Mark Lawson, the* Independent, *30 December 1993*)

Identifying assumptions

We have discussed the two most basic components of arguments – reasons and conclusions – but our understanding of arguments will not be complete unless we can recognize the assumptions upon which an argument relies.

Defining 'assumption'

In order to clarify what is meant by the word 'assumption' in the context of reasoning, let us first consider what we might mean in everyday conversation by talking about 'assuming' something. Suppose you tell me that you are going to the post office before lunch, and I say, 'Take the car, because it will take you too long to walk'. You might reply, 'You're assuming it will take me too long to walk, but you're wrong.' Here you would be referring to something which I have just stated, and telling me that I was mistaken. Hence, everyday usage of the term 'assumption' can imply that an assumption is something which is explicitly asserted, but is not, or may not be, true. One connotation of 'assumption', as people normally use the word, is of a belief that we hold in the absence of strong evidence for its truth – that is to say that the term may mark a distinction between what is known and what is merely believed.

If we interpret the term 'assumption' in this way, we might think that 'assumption' can refer to reasons and conclusions of arguments – that is, to things which have been stated but which may or may not be true. However, those concerned with argument analysis typically make a distinction between reasons, conclusions and assumptions in an argument, and we shall be accepting this distinction here. Moreover, our use of the word will not imply a distinction between what is known and what is merely believed.

For the purpose of our discussion of assumptions in reasoning, we shall use the word 'assumption' to mean something which is taken for granted, but not stated – something which is implicit rather than explicit. It is the fact that an assumption is unstated which distinguishes it from a reason. There may, or may not, be strong evidence for the truth of an assumption of an argument, and this is a characteristic which it has in common with a reason.

Sometimes in the process of evaluating arguments, the term 'presupposition' is used instead of 'assumption'. We prefer the term assumption, because of the possibility of confusion between 'presupposing' and 'supposing'. Usually when arguments tell us to 'suppose that x is true', they are neither stating nor assuming that x *is* true; they are merely exploring what would follow from the truth of x, and often they are doing this precisely in order to show that x must be false. So we must not take the presence of the word 'suppose' in an argument to indicate that an assumption is being made. Indeed, since we are using the term 'assumption' to denote something which is not stated, there are no special words in arguments to indicate the presence of this kind of assumption.

In the sense of 'assumption' set out above, arguments have many assumptions. For each argument we encounter, there will be a whole host of shared background information – for example, the meanings of the words in which the argument is expressed, and general knowledge which gives support to the reasons which are presented. Sometimes these assumptions will be so uncontentious that we will not be interested in making them explicit. Sometimes, however, we will suspect that an argument rests upon a dubious assumption, and it will be important for us to express exactly what that assumption is in order to assess the argument.

We shall say more later about assumptions concerning the meanings of words, assumptions about analogous or comparable situations, and assumptions concerning the appropriateness of a given explanation. But for this chapter, we shall focus on the following two important ways in which assumptions function in an argument: first, in giving support to the basic reasons presented in the argument; second, as a missing step within the argument – perhaps as an additional reason which must be added to the stated reasons in order for the conclusion to be established, or perhaps as an intermediate conclusion which is supported by the reasons, and in turn supports the main conclusion. Let us explore these two uses of assumptions by looking at some examples.

Assumptions underlying basic reasons

The following argument (used in a slightly different form on p. 7 as an example of an argument without a conclusion indicator word) provides an example of the use of an assumption in the first sense, that is to say as something which is intended to support one of the basic reasons of the argument.

> One third of the population still smokes. Everyone must know that smoking causes lung cancer and heart disease. So, knowing the dangers of smoking is not sufficient to stop people from smoking.

This piece of reasoning presents two (basic) reasons for its conclusion:

> Reason 1 One third of the population still smokes.

> Reason 2 Everyone must know that smoking causes lung cancer and heart disease.

In such arguments, the basic reasons may be well-established facts, or they may make the kind of factual claim which we could easily check. Reason 1 seems to be of this nature – that is to say that either it is a generally accepted fact, backed up by reliable statistics, or the author of the argument has made an error about the statistics, and the fraction of the population who smoke is something other than one third. But we do not need to worry about the reasonableness or unreasonableness of assumptions in relation to reason 1, because we would be able to check the correct figure, and in any case, the exact figure is not crucial to establishing the conclusion. Provided that *some* of the population still smoke – and our own experience confirms the truth of this – and provided reason 2 is true, then reason 1, taken together with reason 2, gives support to the conclusion.

Reason 2, however, seems a less straightforward factual claim than reason 1. What lends support to this statement? The claim that 'everyone *must* know . . . ' suggests that there is an underlying reason for expecting people to be well-informed on this topic, and the obvious candidate is that there has been widespread publicity on the dangers to health of smoking – on television, in newspapers and by means of posters in the waiting-rooms of doctors and hospitals. Yet, the move from the doubtless true claim – that there has been publicity about the dangers – to the further claim – that everyone must know about the dangers – depends upon an assumption that everyone has absorbed this information, is capable of understanding the messages which are being put across, and accepts the truth of those messages.

This may seem a reasonable assumption to make, but there may well be those who would wish to challenge it by pointing out that, despite publicity campaigns, some people may not believe that there is a causal link between smoking and ill-health, because they think that the statistics are inconclusive. Even if you do not regard this assumption as controversial, the example illustrates the way we can attempt to identify potentially controversial assumptions underlying the basic reasons presented in an argument. Clearly the identification of such assumptions is closely associated with evaluating the truth of reasons, which will be discussed further in the next chapter.

Another example of assumptions which underlie basic reasons is provided by the passage below:

> Occupational accidents will never be eliminated because all human activity entails risk. But the total number of accidents could be greatly reduced, and the surest way of achieving such a reduction is to penalize, with fines or even imprisonment, those employers on whose premises they occur. Such a policy might result in cases of individual injustice, but it would be effective in securing safer workplaces.

Before reading on, ask yourself what this passage is recommending, and why.

The passage is recommending the imposition of penalties on employers on whose premises occupational accidents occur, on the grounds that this would be the best way to reduce the number of such accidents. There is an obvious unstated assumption here that the threat of penalties would influence the behaviour of employers. But there is a further assumption, since the existence of penalties would not reduce the number of accidents if it were beyond the power of employers to prevent some of the accidents which now occur. So the argument assumes that it is possible for employers to take measures which will prevent the occurrence of some accidents.

Both these assumptions function as reasons which need to be taken together in order to support the claim that the threat of penalties would reduce accidents; and both are reasonable assumptions to make. However, even with these assumptions, the conclusion is too strong, since nothing has yet been said to support the idea that introducing penalties is the *surest* way of achieving a reduction in accidents. So there is yet another assumption – that no other method would be as effective in reducing the number of accidents – and this assumption is more controversial than the others, since it may be possible to get employers to take appropriate action by offering them incentives.

Assumptions as unstated reasons or conclusions

The second type of assumption is one which is needed to fill a gap within the argument, either as an additional reason, without which the reasons which *are* offered do not fully support the conclusion, or as a missing link between the reasons and the conclusion. Here is an example of an argument which illustrates the former:

> In tests designed to investigate the effect of a time delay on recalling a list of words, subjects remembered fewer words after a 30-second delay than after a 10-second delay. Therefore, after a 60-second delay, we would expect subjects to remember even fewer words than after a 30-second delay.

Before going on, ask yourself what is being assumed. Write down any assumption you can identify.

The argument gives just one reason for its conclusion that subjects can be expected to remember fewer words after a 60-second delay than after a 30-second delay. The reason is the piece of evidence that fewer words are remembered after 30 seconds than after 10 seconds. But this piece of evidence supports the conclusion only if it is true that the ability to recall goes on declining after a 30-second delay. So the argument is relying on this assumption in order to draw its conclusion. If we did not make this assumption explicit, we might happily accept the conclusion as obviously following from the evidence. Even when the assumption has been identified, we may consider it a reasonable assumption to make. Nevertheless, it is possible that subjects would be able to remember just as many words after 60 seconds as after 30 seconds, perhaps because the number of words still retained in the memory was a manageable number for the memory to hold. Self-respecting psychologists would not be prepared to draw a firm conclusion without carrying out an appropriate further test.

Here is another example in which one of the reasons has been left unstated:

> If cigarette advertising were banned, cigarette manufacturers would save the money they would otherwise have spent on advertising. Thus, in order to compete with each other, they would reduce the price of cigarettes. So, banning cigarette advertising would be likely to lead to an increase in smoking.

Before reading further, think about the reasoning in this passage. What conclusion is it trying to get us to accept? What basic reason does it offer? Is there an intermediate conclusion? Can you identify a stage in the argument which has not been stated?

The argument starts with a basic reason:

> If cigarette advertising were banned, cigarette manufacturers would save the money they would otherwise have spent on advertising.

From this it draws the conclusion (an intermediate conclusion):

> Thus, in order to compete with each other, they would reduce the price of cigarettes.

It then draws the main conclusion:

> So, banning cigarette advertising would be likely to lead to an increase in smoking.

The main conclusion would not follow from the intermediate conclusion if a reduction in the price of cigarettes made no difference to the numbers of cigarettes bought and smoked. So an assumption underlies this move – that if cigarettes were cheaper, smokers would smoke more, or non-smokers would become smokers. The conclusion does not say exactly what it means by 'an increase in smoking', so we cannot be sure whether the assumption is:

> If cigarettes were cheaper, smokers would smoke more,

or

> If cigarettes were cheaper, more people would smoke,

or perhaps both of these. However, it clearly requires at least one of these assumptions in order to support the conclusion, and perhaps both assumptions are questionable. This is a case of an assumption which, taken together with an intermediate conclusion, gives support to the main conclusion of the argument.

In some pieces of reasoning, an intermediate conclusion may be left unstated. Imagine the following report being made by a policeman to his superior officer about a theft from an art gallery:

> The burglar must have left by the fire escape. This person is not in the building now, but has not been seen leaving the building, and there are guards posted at each entrance.

What intermediate conclusion is the policeman drawing which he has not actually stated? Is this a reasonable conclusion to draw?

The policeman gives three reasons which, taken together, are intended to support the conclusion that the burglar must have left by the fire escape:

> Reason 1 This person is not in the building now

supports the claim that the burglar must have left the building. But

> Reason 2 [the person] has not been seen leaving, and

> Reason 3 there are guards posted at each entrance

do not entitle us to conclude that the burglar must have left by the fire escape unless we assume that reason 3 supports an intermediate conclusion to the effect that no-one could leave undetected except by the fire escape. This assumption, taken together with reasons 1 and 2, give strong support to the conclusion. However, the assumption itself is open to dispute. Perhaps the guards were insufficiently watchful, or failed to recognize the burglar as a burglar, or perhaps it is possible for someone to leave the building undetected through a window on the ground floor.

In the above examples, we have often found that identifying an assumption has led us to question the truth of that assumption, and perhaps to reserve judgement on an argument until we have obtained further evidence or information. But sometimes when we have identified an assumption, we will see that there is no reason at all to think it is true, and we will therefore judge that the argument does not give strong support to its conclusion. Consider the following example:

> Some people say that the depiction of violence on television has no effect on viewers' behaviour. However, if what was shown on television did not affect behaviour, television advertising would never influence viewers to buy certain products. But we know that it does. So it cannot be true that television violence does not affect behaviour.

See if you can pick out the missing assumption here, and say what is wrong with it.

At first sight, this looks like a plausible argument, and many people will be tempted to accept that it is successful in establishing its conclusion. Yet, whichever way we interpret it, it rests on a dubious assumption. One way of interpreting it is to see it as relying on the assumption that, on the one hand, the depiction of violence on television and, on the other hand, advertising on television are alike in important ways – indeed, in ways which allow us to conclude that if one affects the behaviour of viewers, the other one must also affect the behaviour of viewers. But the only thing which they have in common which is *mentioned* in the argument is that both are shown on television.

Perhaps they are alike in some respects, for example, in that they are dramatic, and likely to make an impact on viewers in such a way that viewers remember them. But perhaps the differences between them make a difference to their effects on viewers' behaviour. They are different in that programmes depicting violence are not trying to *sell* violence, not trying to make it attractive to the viewer. There may also be a difference in that most people's natural response to violence is not one of approval, whereas they may well approve of and aspire to some of the lifestyles depicted in advertisements. So the assumption that the two are alike in ways which are relevant to their possible effects on viewers' behaviour is questionable.

There are two other possible interpretations of the passage, each of which rests on a dubious assumption. It *may* be suggesting that because television advertising affects viewers' behaviour, *everything* shown on television, including depictions of violence, must affect behaviour. In that case, the dubious assumption is that if one aspect of television output affects behaviour, all aspects must. Alternatively, it *may* be suggesting that the example of advertising demonstrates that *some* things shown on television affect behaviour. In that case, in drawing its conclusion, it relies on the wholly implausible assumption if some things which are shown on television affect behaviour, then violence shown on television must be one of those things.

The discovery that this argument does not give strong support to its conclusion does not establish that its conclusion is false. Perhaps violence shown on television does affect viewers' behaviour, but, if this is so, it is a truth which cannot be established by means of this particular argument. The ability to identify the mistakes in other people's reasoning is a valuable skill which will be discussed in more detail in the next chapter.

The examples discussed above have been of specific assumptions relating to the subject matter of particular arguments. There are some assumptions which form the whole context in which an argument is presented, but which may not be made explicit, so that someone unfamiliar with the context will find it more difficult to understand the argument. Consider the following passage:

> It has been claimed that powdered rhinoceros horn has aphrodisiac properties, but scientists investigating its effects have been unable to find any chemical effect on the human nervous system. Also, an experiment was carried out in which 100 people ate powdered rhinoceros horn, and another 100 people ate powdered rice, without knowing what they were eating. Very many more of those who ate the rice reported feeling an increase in sexual arousal than did those who ate the rhinoceros horn. This demonstrates that rhinoceros horn probably does not have aphrodisiac properties.

In describing the experiment, and making the claim about what it demonstrates, this argument does not bother to state that powdered rice is not an aphrodisiac. But we can understand that this is being taken for granted, if we reason as follows:

> 'If rhinoceros horn has aphrodisiac properties, then more people should report an increase in sexual arousal after eating rhinoceros horn than after eating powdered rice, which we know does not have aphrodisiac properties. But this did not happen in the experiment. So rhinoceros horn does not have aphrodisiac properties'.

Someone familiar with the way in which such experiments are carried out – the use of a control group of people with which to compare those on whom the rhinoceros horn is tested, the attempt to eliminate irrelevant psychological effects by keeping subjects ignorant of which substance they are eating – will readily understand why the conclusion is being drawn, and will see that there is an unstated assumption that powdered rice is not an aphrodisiac.

Someone unfamiliar with the context of experiments might find it more difficult to understand what was going on. They might, of course, notice that nothing is said about the aphrodisiac properties of powdered rice, and they might reason as follows:

> Powdered rice either does or does not have aphrodisiac properties. If it does, then the experiment cannot tell us whether rhinoceros horn has no aphrodisiac properties or merely weaker aphrodisiac properties than does powdered rice. If it does not, then the experiment *does* indicate that rhinoceros horn does not have aphrodisiac properties, because if it did have such properties, the number of those reporting an increase in sexual arousal should have been higher amongst those who ate rhinoceros horn than amongst those who ate powdered rice.

However, this is a complex piece of reasoning, and, rather than hitting upon this, readers of the argument might instead imagine a context in which it is not known by the experimenters whether *either* substance has aphrodisiac properties. They might then conclude that the experiment appeared to indicate that both substances had aphrodisiac properties, although the powdered rice had much stronger aphrodisiac properties than the rhinoceros horn. So they might regard the conclusion of the argument as mistaken, even though, provided one assumes that powdered rice is not an aphrodisiac, it is a reasonable conclusion to draw from the evidence.

This is an example, then, of an argument with a specific unstated assumption, which it will be more difficult to identify if one is unfamiliar with the context – the whole set of background assumptions – in which the argument is set. This indicates the value of understanding certain contexts of arguments, and that it is valuable to ask certain questions about any argument which cites experimental evidence – for example, what is the purpose of any comparison which is being made between different groups of people, what differing conclusions could be drawn on the basis of one set of assumptions as opposed to a conflicting set of assumptions?

We have said little here of assumptions about the meanings of words and phrases used in reasoning, but we shall discuss this in greater detail in Chapter 5. The following exercises will enable you to practise the skill of identifying assumptions.

Exercise 6: Identifying someone else's assumptions

Sometimes we may find it more difficult to identify the assumptions underlying our own reasoning than to identify the assumptions upon which others are relying. This exercise aims to make you more aware that there may be unstated beliefs in your own reasoning which others would wish to challenge. Suppose, for example, you were to say that the police force should devote more of their time to patrolling on foot in rural areas and suburbs, and, as your reason for believing this, you said that crime has increased in these areas. Someone may point out to you that you are assuming that the presence of policemen on the streets and country lanes can deter potential criminals from committing crimes.

Work with a partner for this exercise. From the following list, choose a statement with which you agree, and give your partner just one reason why you believe this. Your partner must then try to identify any unstated assumptions upon which your view depends.

1 Smoking in public places should be banned.

2 Boxing is a barbaric activity.

3 People should be allowed to hunt foxes.

4 Coarse fishing is a pointless pastime.

5 The older one gets, the wiser one becomes.

6 Newly qualified drivers should not be allowed to drive on motorways.

7 The pattern of family life has changed in recent years.

8 Schools should be required to provide sex education.

9 Too many new motorways are being built.

10 It was a good idea to set up the National Lottery.

You can continue this exercise choosing your own topics. Choose something which is of general interest, but about which you know people tend to disagree.

Exercise 7: Identifying assumptions in arguments

For each of the following passages, identify any unstated assumptions, and say whether they are:

- assumptions which underlie a basic reason, or
- assumptions which function as an additional reason, or
- assumptions which function as an intermediate conclusion.

1 Men are generally better than women at what psychologists call 'target-directed motor skills', but what the rest of us call 'playing darts'. Many people would say that this is not due to innate biological differences in the brain, but is due to the fact that upbringing gives boys more opportunities to practise these skills. But there must be some innate difference, because even three-year-old boys are better than girls of the same age at target skills.

2 Allowing parents to choose the sex of their children could have serious social costs. There would be a higher percentage of males who were unable to find a female partner. Also, since it is true that 90 per cent of violent crimes are committed by men, the number of violent crimes would rise.

3 When people live in a house for a long period of time, they develop a strong commitment to the local neighbourhood. So the continued fall in house prices may have a beneficial effect. The middle classes will become enthusiastic campaigners for better schools, and against vandalism, traffic congestion and noisy neighbours.

4 If the money has been stolen, someone must have disabled the alarm system, because the alarm easily wakes me if it goes off. So the culprit must be a member of the security firm which installed the alarm.

5 The campaign to eradicate measles has been so successful that many doctors have never seen an actual case. Ironically, this puts those few people who do contract the disease in greater danger than they would have been before. The disease can cause serious complications, and it is difficult to diagnose without previous experience because the symptoms are similar to those of several other diseases.

(*Law School Admission Test, Dec. 1984*)

6 There is a much higher incidence of heart attack and death from heart disease among heavy cigarette smokers than among people who do not smoke. It has been thought that nicotine was responsible for the development of atherosclerotic disease in smokers. It now seems that the real culprit is carbon monoxide. In experiments, animals exposed to carbon monoxide for several months show changes in the arterial walls that are indistinguishable from atherosclerosis.

(*Law School Admission Test, March 1985*)

7 Patients on the point of death, who either died shortly afterwards or were revived, have often reported visions of places of exquisite beauty, intense feelings of peace and joy, and encounters with loved ones who had predeceased them. These experiences clearly suggest that there is life after death. Skeptics often claim that such phenomena are caused by changes in the brain that precede death, because these phenomena resemble certain altered states of consciousness that can be induced by drugs or organic brain disease. This objection fails, however, because most of the patients whose experiences of this nature have been reported were neither drugged nor suffering from brain disease.

(*Law School Admission Test, Oct. 1985*)

8 The growth in the urban population of the USA has put increasing pressure on farmers to produce more food. Farmers have responded by adopting labour-saving technology that has resulted in a further displacement of population to cities. As a result, the farm population, formerly a dominant pressure group in national politics, has lost political power.

(*Law School Admission Test, Feb.1983*)

9 Human beings have the power either to preserve or to destroy wild plant species. Most of the wonder drugs of the past fifty years have come from wild plants. If those plants had not existed, medicine could not have progressed as it has, and many human lives would have been lost. It is therefore important for the future of medicine that we should preserve wild plant species.

10 Thirty years ago the numbers of British people taking holidays in foreign countries were very small compared with the large numbers of them travelling abroad for holidays now. Foreign travel is, and always has been, expensive. So British people must on average have more money to spend now than they did thirty years ago.

Answers to Exercise 7 are given on p. 131.

Exercise 8: Re-working Exercise 5

Re-read the passage for Exercise 5 (p. 22). Identify its conclusion, reasons and unstated assumptions. Compare the list which you originally wrote for Exercise 5 with the unstated assumptions which you have now identified.

Answers to Exercise 8 are given on p. 134.

Chapter 2

Evaluating reasoning

Chapter 2

Summary: Parts of an argument

Let us remind ourselves of the most important points covered in the last chapter:

1 *An argument offers a reason* or reasons in support of a *conclusion.*
2 Conclusions may
   - state a supposed fact ('It is dangerous to drive a car after drinking alcohol') or
   - make a recommendation ('You ought not to drive your car').
3 Some arguments introduce their conclusion with the word 'So' or the word 'Therefore'; some arguments do not contain the words 'So' or 'Therefore'.
4 A conclusion does not have to be the last statement in the argument. *Conclusions can appear anywhere* in the argument.
5 An argument can have *unstated assumptions*, that is, items of information, or ideas, which are not explicitly stated in the argument but upon which the argument relies in order to draw its conclusion.
6 *Arguments can have many different structures,* for example:

- **one reason supporting a conclusion,**
- **two or more reasons which, taken together, support the conclusion,**
- **two or more reasons, each of which independently supports the conclusion,**
- **a reason, or reasons, which support an intermediate conclusion, which is then used, either on its own or with other reasons to support a main conclusion.**

Once we understand both the explicit and the implicit reasoning in a passage, we are in a position to assess whether the reasoning is good. There are two questions involved in this assessment:

- Are the reasons (and any unstated assumptions) true?
- Does the main conclusion (and any intermediate conclusion) follow from the reasons given for it?

The answer to both of these questions must be 'yes' in order for an argument to be a good argument. Let us illustrate this with some simple examples. Here is the first one:

> All the Norwich city buses are red. So if the vehicle you saw wasn't red, it wasn't a Norwich city bus.

In this argument, if the reason is false – that is to say, if it is not true that all the Norwich city buses are red – then the argument cannot establish that any vehicle which is not red is not a Norwich city bus. So it is clear that we need to know whether the reason is true in order to know whether we should accept the conclusion. If the reason is true, then in this example we have a good argument, since the reason supports the conclusion.

By contrast, in our second example the reason does not support the conclusion:

> All the Norwich city buses are red. So if the vehicle you saw was red, it was a Norwich city bus.

Here, even if the reason is true, the conclusion is not established, since the reason establishes only that all the Norwich city buses are red, and *not* that no other vehicles are red. This example illustrates that our second question – as to whether the conclusion follows from the reasons given for it – is also crucial to any assessment of an argument.

Evaluating the truth of reasons and assumptions

Common knowledge

It is obvious that no-one will be in a position to know whether all the reasons presented in all the arguments that they may encounter are true. However, we all have a share in a body of common knowledge, many of us have detailed knowledge about our particular field of work or study, and we have some ideas about whom to trust to give us correct information on subjects which are less familiar to us.

Common knowledge can take us a long way in assessing many of the short arguments we looked at earlier. For example, we noted (p. 25) that in the following argument, it was easy for us to assess the first of the reasons:

> One third of the population still smokes. Everyone must know that smoking causes lung cancer and heart disease. So, knowing the dangers of smoking is not sufficient to stop people from smoking.

We may not know the accuracy of the claim that one third of the population still smokes. But we know that quite a number of people still smoke, because we see them doing so; and the argument only needs to establish that *some* people still smoke, despite knowing the dangers. The second reason – that everyone must know the effects of smoking – is more difficult to assess. We observed that it depends upon an assumption that the publicity about the dangers of smoking has been absorbed by everyone,

Perhaps one way to find out if this is so would be to interview smokers in order to discover whether they believe that smoking is dangerous to health. If we found that many smokers did not believe this, we would have produced a piece of additional evidence which would cast doubt on the conclusion. (We shall say more about evaluating additional evidence in a later section.)

We may sometimes need to assess the truth of statements by relying on other people as authorities, perhaps because being certain about the truth of a particular statement depends upon direct experience, which we lack. For example, we may find ourselves as members of a jury having to assess the evidence of eye witnesses to a crime. We do not have the direct experience of what happened, and we may hear two witnesses describing the events in conflicting ways. Another case in which we may have to rely on authorities is where knowledge depends upon expertise, which we ourselves lack. We may, for example, have to rely on the authority of scientists, because we lack the expertise to carry out for ourselves the experiments which they claim establish the truth of something. Although we cannot guarantee that by relying on the authority of others, we will never be mistaken about anything, there are certain criteria we can use in order to minimize the chances of being misled by other people.

Reliability of authorities

If one of your acquaintances has a record of being untruthful, then you are much more cautious about accepting their statements as true than you would be about believing someone who, you thought, had never lied to you. For example, if someone who always exaggerates about his success with women tells you that at last night's disco several women chatted him up, you will be inclined to be sceptical. The habitual liar is an obvious case of someone whose statements are unreliable. In assessing the reliability of authorities, we have to think about the circumstances which could make it likely that what someone said was untrue.

Of course, people who are not habitual liars may deceive others on occasions. They may do so because they stand to lose a great deal – money, respect or reputation – by telling the truth. So when we have to make judgements about the reliability of people we know to be generally truthful, and about people with whom we are not acquainted, we should bear this consideration in mind. That is not to say that we should assume people are being untruthful, simply because it would be damaging to them if others believed the opposite of what they say. But when we have to judge between two conflicting pieces of information from two different people, we should consider whether one of those people has a vested interest in making us believe what they say. For example, if an adult discovers two children fighting, then each child has a vested interest in claiming that the other started the fight. But the evidence of a third child who observed the fight, but knows neither of the protagonists, could be taken to be more reliable in these circumstances.

If someone was not in a position to have the relevant knowledge about the subject under discussion, then it would be merely accidental if their statements about the subject were true. There are a number of circumstances which prevent people from having the relevant knowledge. The subject under discussion may be a highly specialized subject which is understood only by those who have had appropriate education or training. We would not expect reliable information on brain surgery to be given by people who have had absolutely no medical training. This is why in many areas of knowledge, we have to rely on what experts say. Of course, people who are not experts can read about specialized subjects, and pass on information to us about such subjects, so we do not have to disbelieve people simply because they are not experts. But we would be wise to ask the source of their information. For example, if someone told us that they had read that a new car had better safety features than any other model, we should regard the information as more reliable if it came from a consumer magazine or a motoring association than if it was a report of a comment made by a famous person who owned such a car.

Another circumstance in which someone would not be in a position to have the relevant knowledge would be where eye-witness testimony was crucial, and the person could not have seen clearly what happened – perhaps because of poor eyesight, or perhaps because they did not have a clear line of vision on the incident. In the case of a road accident, for example, we would expect to get a more accurate account of what happened from someone with good vision who was close to the accident and whose view was not obscured in any way, than from someone with poor eyesight, or who was at some distance from the accident, or who was viewing it from an angle, or through trees. Similar considerations would apply in the case of information dependent upon hearing rather than vision.

Someone who aims to tell the truth, and who is in a position to have the relevant knowledge may nevertheless be unreliable because of circumstances which interfere with the accuracy of his or her judgement. For example, emotional stress, drugs and alcohol can affect our perceptions. We can be distracted by other events which are happening concurrently. A parent with fractious children in the car may notice less about a road accident than someone who is travelling alone. We can forget important aspects of what has happened, particularly if some time elapses before we report an incident. In the case of people gathering and assessing evidence, as for example scientists and psychologists do, the accuracy of their observations and interpretations can be affected by their strong expectation of a particular result, or their strong desire to have a particular theory confirmed.

Sometimes when we have evidence from more than one source, we find that two (or more) people agree in their descriptions of events – that is to say, their evidence **corroborates** the statements of others. In these circumstances, unless there is any reason to think that the witnesses are attempting to mislead us, or any reason to think that one witness has attempted to influence others, we should regard corroboration as confirming the reliability of evidence.

Summary

Here is a summary of the important questions to ask yourself about the reliability of evidence and of authorities:

1 ***Is this person likely to be telling a lie, to be failing to give full relevant information, or to be attempting to mislead?***
  - **do they have a record of being untruthful?**
  - **do they have a reason for being untruthful?**
    (Would they gain something very important by deceiving me?
    (Would they lose something very important by telling the truth?)

2 ***Is this person in a position to have the relevant knowledge?***
- **If expert knowledge is involved, are they an expert, or have they been informed by an expert?**
- **If first-hand experience is important, were they in a position to have that experience?**
  (If observation is involved, could they see and hear clearly?)

3 ***Are there any factors which would interfere with the accuracy of this person's judgement?***
- **Was, or is, the person under emotional stress?**
- **Was, or is, the person under the influence of alcohol or drugs?**
- **Was the person likely to have been distracted by other events?**
- **Does the person have a strong desire or incentive to believe one version of events, or one explanation, rather than another?**
- **In the case of first-hand experience of an event, was information obtained from the person immediately following the event?**

4 ***Is there evidence from another source which corroborates this person's statement?***

Evaluating support for conclusions

You have already had some practice in judging whether a conclusion follows from, or is supported by, a given reason. This was what Exercise 3 involved, since you were asked to pick out from three statements the one which could be a reason for accepting the truth of the conclusion. When trying to decide whether conclusions of arguments are established by the reasons presented, you are essentially doing the same thing as you did for Exercise 3, but you may have to take into account more than one reason. You may also have to assess a chain of reasoning, which could involve judging whether an intermediate conclusion follows from some basic reasons, and also whether it in turn supports a main conclusion.

A reason will not support a conclusion if it is not *relevant* to the conclusion. This may seem very obvious, since if a reason is concerned with some topic completely unrelated to the subject matter of the conclusion, it would be clearly mistaken to think that the reason could support the conclusion. However, when we talk about a reason being *relevant* to the conclusion, we do not simply mean that it is about the same topic. What we mean is that the reason, if true, *makes a difference* to the acceptability of the conclusion. Relevance in this sense does not necessarily mean that a *relevant* statement *supports* a conclusion. A statement could be relevant and yet count against the conclusion. If we look again at one of the questions from Exercise 3 on p. 18, we can see an example of this:

Conclusion: Blood donors should be paid for giving blood.

Which of the following, if true, could be a reason for the above conclusion?

(a) The Blood Donor service is expensive to administer.
(b) People who give blood usually do so because they want to help others.
(c) There is a shortage of blood donors, and payment would encourage more people to become donors.

The correct answer to this question is (c), which supports the conclusion by showing that if payment were offered to blood donors, this could remedy the shortage of donors. But (a) is also relevant to the conclusion, in the sense that it has some bearing on the recommendation to pay blood donors. If the blood donor service is already expensive to administer, then this may be a reason for rejecting the recommendation. Hence (a) does not support the conclusion, it counts against it.

You may find it useful to think about whether reasons are relevant, because if you can quickly spot that a reason is irrelevant, then you will know that it does not support the conclusion. However, the above example shows that the judgement that a reason is relevant is not sufficient to tell you that the reason supports the conclusion. You will still have to think about the way in which it has a bearing on the conclusion.

The strength of support which reasons provide for a conclusion can vary. In the argument on p. 36, for example, the reason gives the strongest possible support to the conclusion. The argument says:

All the Norwich city buses are red. So if the vehicle you saw wasn't red, it wasn't a Norwich city bus.

In this case, if the reason is true, the conclusion *must* be true. Other arguments may provide less strong support, and nevertheless be good arguments. We can have good reason for believing that something will happen in the future based on evidence from the past, or for believing that what is known to be true of a number of cases will be true of another similar case. For example, we could have good reason to believe that a new car will be reliable, based on the knowledge that most other cars of that model have been reliable. It is not possible to be precise about degrees of strength of support, and in many cases we may need to find out more about the context of an argument in order to assess whether the reasons give strong, fairly strong or only weak support for the conclusion.

In addition to differences in the strength of arguments, there are also different ways in which reasons can support their conclusions. We have already mentioned arguments which use past experience as evidence for their conclusion, and arguments which draw their conclusions on the basis of what is true of similar cases. We are not going to review all of the ways in which arguments can support their conclusions, because it is not particularly important that you should be able to classify arguments into different types. What is important is that you should ask yourself the following questions about the argument:

1 Are the reasons/evidence relevant to the conclusion?
2 If so, do the reasons/evidence provide a good basis for accepting the conclusion?
3 If the conclusion recommends some action or policy, would it be reasonable to act on the basis of the reasons/evidence?
4 Can I think of any other evidence, not mentioned in the argument, which would weaken or strengthen the conclusion?

Let's put this into practice with a few examples. Consider the following argument:

> You ought to take a Happitum travel sickness pill when you go on the ferry. They are very effective against sea-sickness, and you have always been sick in the past when you've travelled by sea.

In this example, it is easy to see that the reasons, if true, give fairly strong support to the conclusion. If you have always been sick on sea crossings, then past experience suggests that you are likely to be sick this time, unless you can prevent this, perhaps by taking some effective drug. So it would be reasonable to act on the evidence that Happitum is effective in preventing sea-sickness. Of course, there may be other considerations, not mentioned in the argument, which would count against the conclusion. If, for example, Happitum had serious side-effects, then it might be more sensible to endure sea-sickness rather than risk ill-health from the drug. Or maybe there are techniques for combating sea-sickness (for example, staying on deck and breathing deeply), which are likely to be effective, and which are less unpleasant than taking a drug.

Here is another example:

> New drugs have been developed which can combat the body's tendency to reject transplanted organs. In the past, most of the deaths which have occurred shortly after heart transplant operations have been due to rejection. So it is likely that these new drugs will improve the survival rate of heart transplant patients.

Are the reasons relevant to the conclusion? Yes, since if most deaths of heart transplant patients have been caused by organ rejection, then the use of drugs which counteract rejection is likely to enable some patients to survive who would have died without the drugs. The reasons are not only relevant to the conclusion, they give it strong support, since if some patients survive who would otherwise have died, this means that the survival rate is higher. There may, of course, be evidence not presented here which would count against the conclusion, for example, if the drugs were highly toxic. But on the assumption that the drugs have been tested for toxicity, and found to be relatively safe, we can regard the conclusion as well supported by the reasons.

Let's look at one more example:

> Introducing an extra written test for learner drivers in the UK will do nothing to reduce the high accident rate amongst drivers aged 17 to 21, because it will not improve their driving skills. In Portugal, every aspiring driver has to have five weeks' theoretical instruction and a stiff examination before he or she is legally entitled to touch the wheel, but this does not result in a low accident rate amongst new drivers. The test is regarded by most as a bureaucratic hurdle to be jumped and forgotten about as soon as possible. All it indicates is that the candidate can read and write. It has no bearing on his or her ability to drive.

This argument uses evidence from Portugal in order to draw a conclusion about what is likely to happen in the United Kingdom. Its major reasons:

> In Portugal, every aspiring driver has to have five weeks' theoretical instruction and a stiff examination before he or she is legally entitled to touch the wheel, but this does not result in a low accident rate amongst new drivers

and:

> [the test] has no bearing on his or her ability to drive.

are offered in support of the conclusion that:

> Introducing an extra written test for learner drivers in the UK will do nothing to reduce the high accident rate amongst drivers aged 17 to 21, because it will not improve their driving skills.

We need to ask first whether the reasons are relevant to the conclusion. Remember that we are not questioning the truth of the reasons at this stage. We are considering whether, assuming the reasons to be true, they support the conclusion.

So, if it's true that the written test in Portugal does not produce a low accident rate amongst new drivers, and that it has no bearing on driving ability, is this relevant to the claim that such a test in the UK will have no impact on the accident rate amongst drivers aged 17 to 21? Well it certainly is a piece of evidence which is worth taking into account, since it is one example of a test which has not had the result which is perhaps hoped for in the UK. But when we consider whether the evidence gives us sufficient basis for accepting and acting upon the conclusion, a number of further questions come to mind. Is there any evidence from other countries besides Portugal?

Are the accidents in this age group (both in the UK and in Portugal) attributable mainly to the driver's lack of skill, or perhaps to the driver's reckless attitude? Are there any cultural differences which might give a test greater impact on attitudes amongst young drivers in the UK than it has amongst their counterparts in Portugal? There is insufficient evidence in this argument to give strong support to the conclusion.

Identifying flaws in reasoning

If the reasons which are presented in an argument do not support the conclusion at all, then the argument has a *flaw*. The skill of identifying flaws in reasoning is being able to see that the conclusion does not follow from the reasons or evidence, and being able to say *why* it does not follow.

Example 1: Some does not imply all

In Chapter 2, when discussing assumptions, we presented the following example of an argument:

> Some people say that the depiction of violence on television has no effect on viewers' behaviour. However, if what was shown on television did not affect behaviour, television advertising would never influence viewers to buy certain products. But we know that it does. So it cannot be true that television violence does not affect behaviour.

One way of summarizing this piece of reasoning is:

1 Television advertising affects viewers' behaviour.
2 So, what is shown on television affects viewers' behaviour.
3 So, violence shown on television must affect viewers' behaviour.

Statement 1 is a basic reason from which statement 2 is meant to follow.

If we take statement 2 as meaning that *some* of what is shown on television affects behaviour, then it does follow from statement 1, because television advertising *is* some of what is shown on television. However, statement 2 interpreted in this way does not support statement 3, as it is intended to, because violence might be one of the things shown on television which does not affect behaviour. If, on the other hand we interpret statement 2 as meaning that *everything* shown on television affects behaviour, then it does not follow from statement 1, because there is no reason to think that just because one thing shown on television affects behaviour, everything else shown on television will do the same. So, whichever way we interpret statement 2, this is not a good piece of reasoning, because it does not give good grounds for the conclusion it draws.

If we are asked to say what the flaw in the reasoning is, we could express it as follows:

> The fact that *some things* which are shown on television affect viewers' behaviour is not a good reason for thinking that violence shown on television must affect viewers' behaviour,

or:

> The fact that *advertising* shown on television affects viewers' behaviour is not a good reason for accepting that *everything* shown on television affects viewers' behaviour.

The ability to state flaws in this way is an important skill to develop, because it can be an effective way of showing other people that there is something wrong with their reasoning. Note that we have stated this flaw without ever considering whether the basic reason – that television advertising affects viewers' behaviour – is true. If we can identify flaws in reasoning, then we can often be satisfied that a particular piece of reasoning does not establish its conclusion, without needing to dispute the truth of the claims upon which the conclusion is based.

We noted in our earlier discussion of the above example that another way of interpreting the argument was to see it as assuming, unjustifiably, that television advertising and violence shown on television were comparable, or analogous, in all relevant or important respects. When assessing arguments, it is useful to look out for analogies or comparisons, and to consider whether the two things which are being compared really are alike in ways which are relevant to the conclusion which is being drawn. This was evident in our discussion on pp. 43–44 of the argument about written tests for learner drivers in Portugal and the United Kingdom.

Example 2: Insufficient evidence

Let us consider another example:

> If people became healthier as the affluence of the country increased, we would expect the population to be healthier now than it was thirty years ago. But over the last thirty years new illnesses, such as chronic fatigue syndrome, have appeared, and we have become more vulnerable to old diseases such as heart disease, strokes and cancer. So the increased wealth of the country has not produced improvements in the health of the population.

The first thing to do when we want to assess whether an argument is flawed is to sort out what the conclusion is, and what evidence or reasons are offered for it. Before reading on, identify the conclusion and the reasons in this passage.

The conclusion, signalled by the word 'So' which introduces the last sentence, is:

> the increased wealth of the country has not produced improvements in the health of the population.

The evidence offered for this is that over a period during which the wealth of the country has increased, new diseases have appeared, and certain old diseases have become more common. Here is a more detailed analysis of the reasoning. There are two strands. First:

> *Basic reason 1*: Over the last thirty years new illnesses, such as chronic fatigue syndrome, have appeared, and we have become more vulnerable to old diseases such as heart disease, strokes and cancer.

This is intended to support an unstated:

> *Intermediate conclusion*: There have been no improvements in the health of the population over the last thirty years.

The second strand is as follows:

> *Assumption (unstated)*: The affluence of the country has increased over the last thirty years.

This gives support to:

> *Basic reason 2*: If people became healthier as the affluence of the country increased, we would expect the population to be healthier now than it was thirty years ago.

The intermediate conclusion and basic reason 2 are then taken together to support the main conclusion. Before reading on, ask yourself whether any of the moves in this reasoning are flawed. Do you accept that the intermediate conclusion follows from basic reason 1, that basic reason 2 follows from the unstated assumption, and that the main conclusion follows from the intermediate conclusion together with basic reason 2?

Remember that when we are looking for flaws, we are not considering whether the reasons are true. So, we do not ask, 'Is it true that the wealth of the country has increased over the last thirty years?' and 'Is it true that new diseases have appeared, and certain old ones have become more common?'. We say instead, 'Even if these claims are true, do they give adequate support to the conclusion that the increased wealth of the country has not produced improvements in the health of the population?' It is clear that they do not give adequate support, because we have not been given much information about the general health of the population. It may be true that there is more vulnerability to heart disease, strokes and cancer, but perhaps some 'old' diseases, for example tuberculosis and bronchitis, are much less common.

Perhaps people have longer lives than was the case thirty years ago, and perhaps they are relatively healthy for long periods of their lives, before succumbing in old age to heart disease, strokes or cancer. There is a problem of interpretation here – what exactly is meant by 'the health of the population'? If we assume that it refers to the percentage of people's lives during which they are free from illness, then we have insufficient information upon which to base the conclusion.

Now we must state concisely what the flaw is:

> Even if some new diseases have appeared and some old diseases have become more common during the last thirty years, it does not follow that the population is less healthy than it was thirty years ago, because people may have long periods of good health before suffering from these diseases.

Note that the flaw occurs in the move from basic reason 1 (the claim about prevalence of diseases) to the unstated intermediate conclusion (that the population is less healthy now than thirty years ago). Note also that, in establishing that this is a flawed argument, we have *not* established that the main conclusion is false. It may be true that the increased affluence of the country has not produced improvements in the health of the population. This could be true if, as the argument tries to suggest, there have been no improvements in the health of the population. But it could be true even if there have been improvements in the health of the population, because those improvements might have occurred even if the country had not become more affluent. So someone aiming to counter the original conclusion in the way set out in Example 3 would also be producing a flawed argument.

Example 3: Correlation not cause

Making a connection between health and affluence, someone might reason:

> There have been improvements in the health of the population over the past thirty years, a period during which there has been an increase in the affluence of the country. So the increased affluence of the country has produced the improvements in the health of the population.

The question as to whether increased affluence has or has not produced improvements in the health of the population cannot be settled without more evidence – evidence both about the incidence of all illnesses in the population, and about whether any improvements in health could not have occurred without greater affluence. The argument simply assumes, without producing any evidence for it, that because two things have occurred together, one of them must have caused the other.

This unwarranted assumption of a causal connection often occurs when someone discovers a correlation – that is, a connection between *x* and *y* such that whenever you find *x*, you are likely to find *y*, or such that whenever a person or a population has characteristic *x*, they are likely to have characteristic *y*. For example, suppose you find that children who frequently watch violent videos are likely to be aggressive; this may be because watching violent videos causes children to be aggressive, or it may be because having a natural tendency to aggressive behaviour causes children to enjoy watching violent videos. Or suppose you find that people who have a great deal of tooth decay are likely to be overweight. This may be because a third factor – perhaps eating large amounts of sugary foods – causes both these conditions. All that you have found when you have discovered a correlation is that two things occur together. This may be because *x* causes *y*, or because *y* causes *x*, or because *x* and *y* are both caused by something else; or it may be simply coincidence. You are guilty of flawed reasoning if you just assume, without further evidence, that *x* causes *y*.

Summary: How an argument can be flawed

We have now seen four different ways in which an argument can be flawed. In Example 1, on the effects of television violence, one interpretation of the argument was flawed because *it drew a general conclusion* about the effects of television *from just one case* (advertising) of which the effects were claimed to be known. The flaw in the other interpretation of the argument was that *it relied on an inappropriate analogy* or comparison. In Example 2, the original argument about increased affluence and health, the argument was flawed because *it drew its conclusion on the basis of insufficient evidence* (the evidence that *some* old diseases are more prevalent), whilst at the same time *failing to look for other relevant evidence* (for example, the reduced incidence of some diseases, the percentage of people's lives during which they are free of illness, and so on). In Example 3, claiming that increased affluence had produced an improvement in the health of the population, the argument was flawed because *it assumed that because two things have occurred together, one has caused the other, and because it failed to consider other possible causes* of the improvements in the health of the population.

The summary shows just some of the ways in which arguments can be flawed. In order to become skilled in identifying flaws in arguments, it is necessary to practise on numerous arguments on a wide range of subject matter. The next exercise offers some practice of this kind. Remember that you are to focus simply on the skill of identifying flaws, and you should not worry in this exercise about whether the reasons are true. Bear in mind the following points:

1 Identify the main conclusion.
2 Identify the reasons and the way they are meant to support the main conclusion.
3 For each step of the argument, ask 'Does this (main or intermediate) conclusion follow from the reasons which are given for it'?
4 Explain why the conclusion does not follow – that is, think of a reason why the conclusion *might not* be true, even if the reason(s) given are true.

Exercise 9: Identifying flaws

Identify the flaws in the following pieces of reasoning.

1 A fantastic basketball team could be created if the best player from each of the best teams formed a new club. Basketball would then become an exciting game for fans everywhere.

(*Law School Admission Test, Oct. 1985*)

2 Crimes and outrages of all sorts have been committed under a full moon by a wide variety of people. The advice to derive from this is clear: when the moon is full, trust no-one, not even yourself.

(*Law School Admission Test, Sept. 1984*)

3 Young people today have more formal education than their grandparents had. Wilma is young, so she must have more formal education than her grandparents had.

(*Law School Admission Test, 1982*)

4 Neither marijuana nor LSD can be harmful, since they are used by doctors to ease the pain of cancer patients.

(*Law School Admission Test, 1982*)

5 Adolescents frequently suffer from anaemia, but this is not, as is often supposed, due to insufficient iron in their diets, but is a result of this group's having a higher requirement for iron than that of the rest of the population.

(*Law School Admission Test, Feb. 1983*)

6 We know that diet is an important cause of disease. One example of a disease which is attributable to diet is the heart attack, which is so common in Western countries. In countries with different diets, the diseases differ also. For example, in Japan the most common fatal diseases are strokes and cancers of the stomach. The Japanese diet has a much lower fat content and a much higher fibre content than the Western diet. So if people in the West were to adopt a Japanese low-fat/high-fibre diet, they would be unlikely to die from heart attacks. They would die instead from

the diseases which are common in Japan – that is to say, strokes and cancers of the stomach.

7 Who invented cooking? Since cooking requires heat, the first cooks must have used fire. Until recently, there was no evidence of fire having been used earlier than 200,000 years ago. But now, reliable scientific evidence has shown that the ancestors of *Homo Sapiens* were lighting fires almost 400,000 years ago. So cooking must have been invented at that time.

8 The witness said that he had seen Fred in the vicinity of the shop at the time the fire was started. But we know this witness has a grudge against Fred, and he has been known to give unreliable evidence in the past. So we cannot rely on this person's statement. Hence Fred must have been somewhere else when the fire was started.

9 Most people could be musical geniuses if they practised hard enough. A psychologist interested in whether genius is mainly hard work rather than inspiration has examined the lives of 76 composers. Most of them had at least a decade of painstaking training before they wrote any masterpieces. Mozart, for example, was drilled incessantly by his father in techniques of composition before he composed his first work of genius at the age of 12.

10 Some people claim that poverty is one of the causes of crime. But there can't be any kind of link between being poor and committing crimes, because lots of people who are poor never commit a crime.

Answers to Exercise 9 are given on p. 137.

Evaluating further evidence

Often when we present a case to someone else for accepting a particular conclusion, they will say, 'Ah, but what about . . . ?', offering some piece of information which we have not mentioned and which they think weakens our case. In relation to our earlier example on the dangers of smoking, imagine someone saying to you, 'Knowing that smoking is dangerous cannot be sufficient to stop people from smoking, because there has been so much publicity about the health risks, and yet people still smoke.' Let us suppose that a survey of smokers' beliefs has been carried out. You might then reply to the above statement, 'Ah, but what about that survey which showed that, unlike non-smokers, smokers generally believe that smoking is *not* bad for one's health?' The other person must then consider what impact this has on their conclusion.

Being able to assess the impact of additional evidence is valuable because people frequently challenge each others' reasoning by offering some new piece of information. One response to such challenges would be to question the truth of the new piece of evidence, and this would involve one of the skills we have already mentioned – that of evaluating the truth of evidence or reasons. Another response might be to say that even if the new piece of evidence were true, it would not weaken the conclusion. This involves the other vital skill which we have discussed – that of assessing the degree of support which a reason gives to a conclusion.

Of course, the context may not be one in which we are trying to defend a conclusion – nor should we be thinking in terms of the necessity to defend a conclusion at all costs. That would be to indulge in uncritical thinking – being determined to believe something even in the face of evidence to the contrary. So we must be prepared to acknowledge that sometimes additional evidence will weaken our conclusions. Sometimes new evidence comes to light not in the context of a discussion, not when someone else is trying to undermine one's own reasoning, but simply in relation to a subject upon which we already hold an opinion, and believe that we hold that opinion for good reasons. Once we see that the new evidence is relevant to the issue, we must then consider whether it counts for or against our earlier opinion – that is to say we must consider whether it *strengthens* our reasoning and not merely whether it *weakens* it.

Exercise 10: Further evidence

This exercise gives you practice in evaluating the impact of additional evidence on an argument. For each of the following multiple choice questions, pick the correct response, explain why it is the correct response, and explain why each of the other responses is incorrect.

1 A recent study found that school-age children who participate in school-related sports activities fight less during school and school-related activities than do those children who do not participate. It was concluded that sports must satisfy an aggressive impulse which would otherwise be released through fighting.

Which of the following, if true, weakens the conclusion referred to in the above passage?

(a) School-related sports activities are always supervised by adults.
(b) Supervisors of school-related sports activities discourage participants from being extremely aggressive.
(c) Children who participate in school-related sports activities tend to be more aggressive physically than those who do not participate.
(d) Approximately 85 per cent of the fights children get into during school or school-related activities take place during break times.

(e) Most schools suspend those who fight during school or school-related activities from the schools' sports teams.

(*Law School Admission Test, 1982*)

2 Although the number of undergraduates studying engineering has grown greatly over the last five years, there may be a shortage of engineering teachers in the near future because the number of people receiving PhDs in engineering, those most likely to teach, has not been increasing. This results because the high salaries offered to engineers without advanced degrees reduce the incentive to pursue postgraduate studies. Therefore, businesses will have to recognize that their long-term interests would best be served by reducing salaries for those without advanced degrees.

Which of the following, if true, would *most* weaken the above argument?

(a) Enrolment in the sciences has grown over the last five years.
(b) Fewer than half of the people who have received PhDs in engineering teach full-time.
(c) Businesses pay high salaries to engineers with advanced degrees.
(d) The increases in engineering enrolment are due to the high salaries paid by businesses.
(e) Many university programmes are funded by businesses interested in engineering research.

(*Law School Admission Test, Dec. 1983*)

3 *Joan*: One method of reducing serious crime in the United States is to adopt the English system of providing free heroin to heroin addicts.
Anna: That's absurd. It's just like giving free cars to automobile thieves.

Which of the following, if true, would *most* strengthen Joan's argument?

(a) Heroin addicts are more likely to be violent under the influence of drugs than when they are anticipating using those drugs.
(b) The amount of money needed annually to supply heroin to heroin addicts is less than the amount lost annually by the victims of drug-related crimes.
(c) It is cheaper to provide addicts with drugs than to jail them after they have committed crimes.
(d) The amount of serious crime committed by non-addicts is roughly equal in England and the United States.
(e) A substantial amount of serious crime is committed by heroin addicts in order to support their habits.

(*Law School Admission Test, Oct. 1983*)

4 Since only four per cent of all automobiles fail the state's annual safety inspection solely because of defective direction indicators, the state's automobile association recommends that direction indicators no longer be inspected. Although they are an important safety feature, too few are defective to make the expense of testing them worthwhile.

Which of the following, if true, points out the *most* serious weakness in the recommendations of the automobile association?

(a) Owners will no longer maintain their direction indicators in working order if the inspection requirement is dropped.
(b) Owners of vehicles with defective direction indicators may not have learned to use manual direction signals.
(c) Eliminating the inspection of the direction indicators will make the state's inspection procedure less thorough than those of neighbouring states.
(d) Vehicles with defective direction indicators will fail inspection anyway if they have other safety defects.
(e) Vehicles that have defective direction indicators may have other defects not covered by the safety inspection system.

(*Law School Admission Test, Feb. 1983*)

5 A recent study found that if children watched up to one hour of television a day, their performance in school was unaffected, but if they watched between two and three hours a day, they were likely to perform considerably less well than their peers who watched less. The researchers concluded that if parents carefully monitored the time their children watched television, the children's school performance would be maintained at adequate levels.

If true, which of the following statements about the children in the study would *most* strengthen the conclusions of the researchers?

(a) Most of the children who performed at below average levels in school watched more than two hours of television a day.
(b) Children who watched television mostly at weekends performed better in school than children who watched television mostly on school nights.
(c) Children who spent more time reading than watching television performed better in school than those who did not.
(d) The disparities among the children in terms of school performance lessened when the television viewing habits of the children became more uniform.
(e) The children who reduced the amount of television they watched daily spent the extra time reading.

(*Law School Admission Test, Dec. 1985*)

6 It is unwise to continue the career training and employment programmes administered in most prisons today. These programmes do not achieve what they are meant to achieve because most ex-prisoners choose not to pursue the occupations they followed during the time they spent in prison.

Which of the following, if true, *most* weakens the above argument?

(a) Many habits and skills learnt in prison training programmes are valuable in a great variety of occupations.

(b) Prisons have an obligation to provide prisoners with occupational training they will later use in employment.
(c) Prison career training programmes tend to make prisoners more productive during their time in prison.
(d) Training prisoners for future employment is a major goal of most rehabilitation programmes today.
(e) In most prisons today, prisoners can prepare for their choice of a number of occupations.

(*Law School Admission Test, 1986*)

7 Certain physiological changes accompany the psychological stress of telling a lie. Reliable lie detection is possible because, with the appropriate instruments, we can measure the physiological symptoms of lying.

Which of the following, if true, *most* weakens the above argument?

(a) Lie detectors are expensive machines, and they require careful maintenance.
(b) Some people find lying only moderately stress-inducing.
(c) Lie detection requires highly trained, capable personnel.
(d) Even the appropriate instrument can be misused and abused.
(e) Numerous kinds of psychological stress produce similar physiological symptoms.

(*Law School Admission Test, March 1984*)

Answers to Exercise 10 are given on p. 139.

Questioning explanations

Some pieces of reasoning, rather than trying to convince us that we should accept a particular conclusion, aim instead to explain something which we already accept as being true. This is a case of giving *reasons why* something is as it is, rather than giving *reasons for* believing something. The difference is illustrated by the following report from the *Independent* of 17 February 1994:

> Latest figures for cancers in England and Wales show an increase of four per cent in 1988. Richard Doll, consultant to the Imperial Cancer Research Fund, said one explanation was the rising number of elderly people.

Richard Doll's comments are not trying to convince us of the fact that cancers increased in 1988. They are taking the truth of that for granted, and trying to explain why this increase occurred.

This is a case of an explanation occurring as an independent piece of reasoning; but we may also find explanations offered within an argument, as part of a longer passage of reasoning. What we need to know about an explanation is whether it is the correct explanation. It may not be easy to settle such a question, but there are strategies we can use to attempt some assessment of an explanation. One is to examine any questionable assumptions underlying the explanation. Another is to think of possible alternative explanations. If we can think of two or three equally plausible explanations of something, then we should be cautious about accepting any of them as the correct explanation until we have further information.

We can try these strategies on the above example, although it may seem presumptuous to question the judgement of a leading authority in cancer research! What assumptions underlie Richard Doll's explanation? If the increase in cancers is attributable to 'rising numbers of elderly people', this must be because people who, had they lived in earlier times, would have died from other diseases (which are now more easily treatable or preventable) are living to an age at which they are likely to get cancer. No doubt further support for this assumption could be found by examining figures on the incidence of cancer in different age groups.

What alternative explanations of the increase in cancer can we suggest? Well, there would be an increase in cancer figures if the population in general were more susceptible to the disease – perhaps because of pollutants in the environment. There would be an increase in the figures if particular groups had a greater incidence of cancer, due to changes in habits and practices. For example, it could be that new medications for circulatory diseases cause more cancers, or that more cancers are caused by more women taking hormone replacement therapy. Light could be shed on the plausibility of these alternative explanations by examining figures on the incidence of cancer amongst different groups. We are not suggesting that Richard Doll's explanation is likely to be incorrect – in fact he is more than likely to have taken all these factors into account before offering his explanation. But the example serves to illustrate the way in which we can question explanations, perhaps reserve judgement on them until we have more information, and perhaps take steps to investigate which of various alternative explanations is the most plausible.

The following passage describes a piece of research which aimed to find out the most plausible explanation of a known fact. It is adapted from an article in the *Independent on Sunday* of 25 June 1995:

> Motorists in their teens and twenties have a low opinion of elderly drivers, whom they regard as bumbling old fools who shouldn't be allowed on the roads.
>
> Some old drivers are indeed incompetent, and data from the USA has shown that the accident rate for drivers rises substantially after the age of 70. A research team at the University of California at Los Angeles has now carried out a detailed study of the abilities of elderly drivers.
>
> The research team recruited volunteers in their early seventies who,

according to their doctors, had signs of early dementia due to Alzheimer's disease, or to narrowing of the arteries. Other drivers of the same age had diabetes as their only medical condition, and a group of younger drivers was used for comparison.

All the drivers – the demented, the diabetics and the young controls – were taken on a drive around a three-mile road network with intersections, speed bumps, traffic signs, signals and parking lots. Each driver's performance was graded by an instructor in the car, which was fitted with an on-board computer which recorded braking speed, steering, crossing the centre line, and so on. The drivers also worked their way through a series of standard tests of mental ability, concentration and short-term memory.

The results showed that the 70-year-olds with diabetes did just as well on the test drives and mental tests as the younger drivers. The drivers with early dementia did worse. They drove slowly, and the mistakes they made were serious – for example, turning into a one-way street marked 'no entry'. The conclusion was that drivers in their seventies in normal health (with normal vision) can perform at a level comparable with young, healthy adults – at least in a suburban, non-stressing environment. Statistics showing that drivers in this age group have high accident rates are, the report says, at least partly attributable to people continuing to drive after they have become mildly demented.

Before reading on, ask yourself the following questions:

- what was the known fact which the study sought to explain?
- what explanation would the author expect young motorists to give?
- what explanation does the report of the study give?

The passage tells us in the second paragraph that data from the USA shows that the accident rate for drivers rises substantially after the age of 70. This is the fact which is to be explained, and it means, of course, that *as a group* the drivers aged over 70 have a higher percentage of accidents than those aged under 70. It is clear from the first paragraph that the author would expect young drivers to explain this fact by saying that *all* drivers aged over 70 are incompetent, and therefore more likely to have accidents. The study did tests to assess the competence of drivers, and found that those aged over 70 who had dementia were less competent than young drivers, but those aged over 70 who did not have this medical condition were no less competent than young drivers.

This suggests that the most plausible explanation of the higher accident rate amongst drivers aged over 70 is that *some* drivers aged over 70 are incompetent due to dementia. We should note that the article suggests that the driving test was conducted in a 'suburban, non-stressing environment'. If this is correct, then, in order to be certain that the explanation offered by the study was the most plausible, we would want some evidence about the competence of both young drivers and drivers aged over 70 in more stressful traffic conditions.

Of course, dividing all drivers into only two groups, over 70 and under 70, obscures any statistical differences in the very large under-70 group – this is an example of how critical of statistics we must be, even when we accept them. For example, drivers under 25 have a significantly higher accident rate than those over 25. Elderly drivers might wish to argue that this showed a high incidence of undiagnosed dementia among young drivers!

Exercise 11: Offering alternative explanations

For each of the following passages, identify which part of the passage is the explanation, and which part is the fact which is being explained. Then suggest an alternative explanation for this fact. Do not worry if you are uncertain whether your explanation is true. Just try to think of something which, if it were true, would be another possible explanation.

1 Public confidence in the police force is declining at the same time as fear of crime is growing. People's lack of confidence in the police is the reason why they are so much more fearful of crime.

2 Why has the divorce rate increased so much over the last thirty years? It is because there are so many more couples these days who are unhappily married.

3 The human race has never received a well-authenticated communication from beings elsewhere in the universe. This is because the only intelligent life in the universe is on our own planet.

4 The number of cars per head of population in Britain continues to rise. This is why, whenever a new road such as the M25 is built, the density of traffic in that area increases.

5 Because the weather was so bad in Britain last summer, the number of people taking holidays in British resorts declined.

Answers to Exercise 11 are given on p. 144.

Exercise 12: Identifying and evaluating explanations

In each of the following three passages, an explanation is offered, or a number of different explanations is considered, for a given fact or phenomenon. For each passage:

(a) identify the fact or phenomenon which is to be explained,
(b) find the explanation or explanations given in the passage,
(c) think of any other possible explanations which are not mentioned in the passage,
(d) either
  - say which explanation you think is the most plausible, and why; or
  - think about further evidence you would need in order to decide which explanation is the most plausible.

This exercise could form the basis of a class discussion.

1 *Girls doing well while boys feel neglected, study finds*

Boys are blamed for everything, complained a 14-year-old, encapsulating the jaundiced view of school that seems to be having such a bad effect on boys' exam results.

It was a myth that girls perform poorly at school, said Michael Younger, whose study of an East Anglian comprehensive elicited the 14-year-old boy's comment. Boys are the problem.

The boy also complained: 'Girls are treated a lot better and get first choice of equipment and task'.

Reflecting the national picture, the girls at this school have done consistently better at GCSE than the boys, although the gap has narrowed.

Mr Younger said some schools should take credit for implementing equal opportunities policies which had reduced discrimination against girls. They now had to tackle boys' under-achievement and disengagement, although Mr Younger admitted that it was a complex problem to which he did not have any easy answers.

He and Molly Warrington, his fellow researcher at Homerton College, Cambridge, found that boys felt they were unfairly treated or neglected in class, although teachers and the majority of girls disagreed.

Staff said boys went to considerable lengths not to appear swotty – for instance, denying to classmates they had done homework even when they had, or playing up in class. They saw boys as unable to concentrate or organise themselves and lacking in motivation.

Girls tended to be more focused, and study was not seen as bad for their image. Parents and teachers agreed that girls did more homework, while boys saw it as a necessary evil to be done as quickly as possible.

Seventy per cent of girls thought female teachers treated boys and girls equally; only 46 per cent of boys agreed.

A majority of all the pupils surveyed thought male teachers were biased towards girls, however – accepting behaviour from girls which they punished in boys.

A fifth-form girl agreed that girls were treated more leniently by male teachers. 'The girls have a reputation for being well-behaved, so if, for example, they don't do their homework they won't get told off as much.'

Boys from the same year complained that they got less attention from male teachers than the girls did.

Girls appeared to have clearer goals, said Mr Younger, which led them to focus on their work. Some boys had no idea what they wanted to do after GCSE and several had no idea what later courses to take.

(Guardian, 26 August, 1995)

2 *Number of road deaths at post-war record low*

Fewer people were killed on Britain's roads last year than in any year since 1926, but a rise in the number of those seriously injured suggests that further improvements are unlikely.

Preliminary figures released by the Department of Transport suggest that 3,651 people died on the roads, a fall of 4 per cent compared with 1993 when 3,814 died – the previous post-war record low.

The fall in deaths, despite an increase in road traffic of 3 per cent, appears to be explained by better paramedic treatment at the roadside and improved medical care, since the figures for serious injuries have increased to 46,784, a rise of 4 per cent.

In fact the number of deaths is just about the only figure to have gone down between 1993 and 1994. Serious injuries for both car users and pedestrians also increased. Indeed pedestrian casualties rose by 2 per cent overall from 1993 levels to 49,026 and while deaths fell by 7 per cent to 1,148, serious injuries increased by 4 per cent to 11,924.

While Britain generally has a good safety record on the roads compared with its European neighbours, the number of child casualties is proportionally higher and last year reinforced the trend, with child casualties going up by 6 per cent to 45,239. The number of child pedestrians killed on the road went up from 135 to 173, a rise of 28 per cent.

Edmund King, campaigns manager of the RAC, said: 'There are very worrying features about these figures, particularly on child deaths. One thing that could be done quite easily is to bring the clocks into line with the Continent so that children would not have to go home from school in the dark'.

He says that the increase in serious injuries shows that the number of accidents is rising and he feels many are caused by drivers feeling too insulated in their modern cars. Mr King said, 'They listen to the stereo, have the heater on and it's almost as if the outside world doesn't exist. And then they fall asleep or make a mistake . . . '

Brigitte Chaudhry, national secretary of RoadPeace, an organisation for road accident victims, said the figures on deaths may be misleading; 'Deaths are only counted as such if they occur within 30 days of the accident. Nowadays, many people are kept alive for much longer thanks to modern medical techniques and die later than that.'

She added that the main reason for the reduction in deaths over the last

30 years is a decline in the number of vulnerable road users, such as pedestrians and cyclists, using the roads: 'As there are fewer pedestrians on the road and more are getting hurt, it suggests that roads are more dangerous and not safer.'

(Independent, *31 March 1995*)

3 *Science debunks miracle of weeping madonna*

The only weeping madonna officially accepted by the Roman Catholic Church has been exposed as a fake by an Italian scientist who used the logic of Mr Spock, the deductive reasoning of Sherlock Holmes and a knowledge of capillary attraction.

There has been a sharp increase in the sightings of weeping madonnas, from Ireland to Croatia, but the only one recognised by the Church is a statue of the Virgin Mary in the town of Siracusa in Sicily. It first began weeping in 1953.

The 'miracle' of a statue that appears to weep has even been caught on film. But Luigi Garlaschelli, a chemistry researcher at the University of Pavia, believes he has an explanation.

Dr Garlaschelli has made his own weeping madonna which baffled onlookers into believing the statue was able to shed tears without any mechanical or electronic aids or the deployment of water-absorbing chemicals.

The secret, he revealed, is to use a hollow statue made of thin plaster. If it is coated with an impermeable glazing and water poured into the hollow centre from a tiny hole in the head, the statue behaves quite normally.

The plaster absorbs the liquid but the glazing prevents it from pouring out. But if barely perceptible scratches are made in the glazing over the eyes, droplets of water appear as if by divine intervention – rather than by capillary attraction, the movement of water through sponge-like material.

Dr Garlaschelli said the actual madonna of Siracusa is kept behind a glass partition and he is unable to inspect its glazing for himself. 'I think permission won't be granted to examine it,' he said. 'Many of these relics are not allowed to be examined. However, examination of a copy from the same manufacturer as the original proved it to be made of glazed plaster and to possess a cavity behind the face.'

(Independent on Sunday, *9 July 1995*)

Answers to Exercise 12 are given on p. 145.

Summarising the skills of evaluation

The skills discussed in this chapter need to be used together when assessing a passage of reasoning. We need to consider whether the reasons, and any unstated assumptions, are true; whether the argument relies upon evidence from anyone whose authority is questionable; whether anything which we ourselves know, but which is not stated in the passage, weakens or strengthens the conclusion; whether, if the passage relies upon an explanation, we can think of equally plausible alternative explanations; and finally whether we can identify flaws in the reasoning which show us that the conclusion is not well supported by the reasons.

Here is a checklist to work through when assessing the reasoning in the passages in Exercise 13:

1 Find the conclusion.
2 Find the reasons and any unstated assumptions.
3 Consider how far you can go in assessing the truth of the reasons and the unstated assumptions. Think about how you would seek further information to enable you to assess the truth of reasons.
4 Does the reasoning rely on evidence from sources whose authority is questionable?
5 Do you yourself have any knowledge which strengthens or weakens the conclusion? (Remember to subject your own 'knowledge' to the same standards of scrutiny as you apply to the claims made by other people!)
6 Does the passage contain any explanations? If so, are they plausible, and are they the only plausible explanations of what is being explained?
7 If you believe that the conclusion is not well supported by the reasons and assumptions, can you state the way in which the move from reasons to conclusion is flawed?

Exercise 13: Practising the skills

Identify and evaluate the reasoning in each of the following passages.

1 The Automobile Association has objected to the idea, floated by the roads minister, to allow drivers on British motorways to 'undertake' – or pass other cars on the left instead of the right.

Yet the minister's diagnosis of the problem is correct. Too often, a driver hugs the right-hand lane of a motorway, and sees no reason to move since he is already travelling at the speed limit or above. Another approaches from behind wanting to pass, but is blocked by the smugly virtuous driver in his path. (The protagonists in such disputes are almost always men.) At best, the result is a locking of horns, lights and brakes; at worst, the faster driver can lose patience and provoke a crash – sometimes with fatal results.

The ideal solution is obvious: for Britons to adopt the rigid discipline common in some parts of continental Europe, where drivers who overtake always return briskly to the lane from which they came. That is the theory here too; but the police seem unable to force drivers to obey the law as it stands.

The minister's solution is second best. Overtaking on both sides works tolerably on congested 55 mph highways in the United States; it allows all lanes on a road to be used to the full, and thus reduces delays and the frustration they cause. As British traffic conditions come more and more to resemble those of the USA, the American solution seems increasingly tempting.

But there are legitimate doubts about whether US habits would work in Britain. Might our higher motorway driving speeds and narrower roads cause more accidents under a US-style system? Might British drivers become confused, resulting in more accidents until things settle down? Only research and consultation with experts, rather than merely with driving organisations, can answer those questions. At the moment, there is little evidence either way.

In the meantime, safety would be improved by a change to the Highway Code obliging drivers not only to indicate before changing lanes, but also to leave their indicators on while they are in the overtaking lane. The flashing indicator would serve as an unaggressive signal to drivers in front to pull over to the left as quickly as they safely can; and it would remind the overtaker to do the same immediately afterwards.

(Independent, *28 September 1993 – adapted*)

2 [The reduction in the price of *The Times* newspaper has] demonstrated a basic maxim of the market system which is neglected by most British business. If you lower your prices, it is very likely that you will *enlarge* the market for your sort of product.

The lesson seems so trite that I am embarrassed to set it out in print. And yet it seems to pass over the heads – or beneath the notice – of almost everyone involved in financial decision making. If the market for a category of thing is static or contracting, the standard British response is to raise prices so as to maintain profit levels. Scarcely anyone seems to consider the possibility that lowering prices by cutting profit margins to the bone can do more than merely redistribute a fixed amount of custom, by actually enticing more people into a market they might otherwise not enter at all. The total number of possible customers is increased by those who might now consider, say, purchasing a quality newspaper at all, or who return to buying such a newspaper every day or perhaps more than one newspaper per day.

The market for most commodities is not set in stone; people's tastes and preferences are not immutable. They will exercise their freedom to choose when given half an economic chance, just as they can be forced to give up things that they like if they become too expensive. With every tax increase on cigarettes, the number of people smoking drops. When London restaurant prices became seriously out of line with spending power, so many people stopped eating out that a great many restaurants closed.

A simple inversion of this principle – cut prices as low as you can and people will buy more – is the prevailing philosophy in countries such as the United States, where supermarkets, for example, expect to run on profit margins of 1 or 2 per cent as opposed to the 8 per cent which is normal in Britain. In what has been described as a gloomy forecast for British food retailers, Tesco has predicted that the industry would be hit by 'intense competition and further pressure on prices' in the coming years.

Well, one man's gloom is another's cheap food. And in the same statement, Tesco's chairman reported that Tesco's sales and profits were both up as a result of – guess what – its 'lower pricing' policy. Just fancy that.

(*Janet Daley, Copyright ©* The Times, *23 September 1993*)

3 Crime figures have certainly risen since the Fifties, but it should be remembered that only 5 per cent of crimes have a violent or sexual content. A quarter of reported crimes are burglaries, vandalism or criminal damage. Figures for crimes of these types have increased, but a great deal of such crime is trivial – 70 per cent of burglaries are of amounts under £100. Some of the increase is to do with increased opportunity – there are more things now for people to steal and vandalise.

People are more inclined to report crime now than they were in the Fifties. Because of insurance, 98 per cent of car crimes are reported. And the physical violence which used to be taken for granted in domestic situations no longer is. So, quite rightly, more of it gets reported. Of the three categories of rape, reports of rape by strangers has barely increased. It's with intimates and acquaintances that it's really gone up.

So now we call everything crime and ask the police to protect us, all the time fostering a myth that the past was much more peaceable. But in some streets in London, you couldn't hang washing out in the Thirties for fear of its being stolen, and there was a fight on the steps outside the pub every Saturday night.

The fears that people have of crime are based on the assumption that the incidence of violent and serious crimes has increased greatly in the past forty to fifty years. But they are mistaken in thinking that the evidence supports this assumption.

(*adapted from an article by David Hare,* Independent on Sunday, *10 October 1993*)

Answers to Exercise 13 are given on p. 146.

Chapter 3

Recognizing implications

Drawing conclusions

One important aspect of reasoning is the ability to go further than the information you have been given, to draw conclusions from evidence, to see what follows from statements which other people make. This is an ability which we all exercise to a certain extent in our daily lives. If we draw back the curtains in the morning, and find that last night's snow covering has gone, we conclude that the temperature must have risen overnight. If we know that a friend has completed a 150-mile car journey in two hours, we conclude that they must have exceeded the 70 mph speed limit.

Sometimes our conclusions will be more tentative than in these two examples. If we know that a colleague's children have all had bad colds recently, and we hear that colleague sneezing throughout the day, then it is reasonable to conclude they have caught a cold. But they may not be suffering from a cold. Perhaps their sneezing is caused by an allergy to something in the office, for example, a new pot plant or a new type of printing ink. In cases like this, where the evidence points to a conclusion which may need to be reconsidered in the light of further evidence, it is best to express our conclusion as something which is 'probable' or 'likely'.

To improve our capacity for critical reasoning, we need

to exercise the ability to draw conclusions in a systematic way whenever we are presented with information – in discussions with others, when reading newspapers and textbooks, when listening to the comments of politicians. We may find it easiest to draw conclusions about those subjects with which we are most familiar, but with practice, we can make progress in improving the ability in relation to less familiar topics.

Let us turn to some examples to illustrate this. Consider the following passage:

> Men with low blood cholesterol levels are more likely to develop intestinal cancer than those with high blood cholesterol levels. But men who have high blood cholesterol levels have an above-average risk of suffering a heart attack.
>
> *(Law School Admission Test, Dec. 1984)*

What conclusions can be drawn from this information? Can we conclude that it would be a good thing for all men to aim to have a low blood cholesterol level, on the grounds that this would reduce their risk of suffering a heart attack? No, not from the information available, because if they achieved a low blood cholesterol level they would be more likely to develop intestinal cancer. So the most which can be concluded is that lowering a patient's blood cholesterol level in order to reduce the risk of heart attack may increase the patient's risk of intestinal cancer, and thus that it may not be wise to attempt to lower a patient's blood cholesterol level.

Note the tentative nature of this conclusion. It is possible that further information might lead us to revise the conclusion. Suppose that intestinal cancer is a disease which usually occurs in old age. In that case, lowering someone's blood cholesterol level may move them out of the group likely to die relatively young from a heart attack, and into the group likely to live much longer, but also at risk of – eventually – developing intestinal cancer. In that case, it may be wise to attempt to lower the blood cholesterol levels of those likely to suffer heart attacks.

Let us look at another example:

> Repeated spraying with the insecticide did not rid the tobacco fields of the insect. Only the strongest of the species survived each spraying. When they mated, they produced offspring more resistant to the insecticide than they were.
>
> *(Law School Admission Test, June 1983)*

What can be concluded from this information? We know that the insects which were strong enough to survive repeated spraying with insecticide produced offspring with even greater resistance to the insecticide. In the original population of insects, there were obviously some with weak resistance and some with strong resistance, so perhaps it is just a matter of chance whether a particular insect has strong or weak resistance, and therefore just a matter of chance that the offspring of the survivors had strong resistance.

But if it were just a matter of chance, then we should expect the new generation to include some insects with weak resistance to the insecticide. The fact that they all had strong resistance suggests that there is something about being the offspring of those with strong resistance which makes insects more likely to have strong resistance. And this suggests that resistance to insecticide, in at least some species, can be passed from one generation of insects to the next. This is a useful conclusion to draw because it tells us that repeated spraying with insecticide may not have the effect of eventually eliminating insect pests. It may even have the effect of making the insect population stronger, if those which have the resistance to the insecticide are strong in other respects as well, for example, in their abilities to reproduce or to withstand adverse weather conditions and disease.

Here are some exercises for you to practise your skill in drawing conclusions.

Exercise 14: Drawing conclusions

For each of the following, say what conclusion you can draw from the passage.

1 The pond is frozen this morning. It was not frozen yesterday.

2 There is a 'flu epidemic sweeping through the school. Gitta, one of the pupils, has a very high temperature and aching muscles, both of which are symptoms of 'flu.

3 The winter has been very severe. When we have a severe winter, the daffodils usually come into flower late.

4 Jane arrived before Jim, although they set off at the same time, and they were both travelling by car.

5 The murder victim died at 9 pm on Saturday. It is suspected that he may have been poisoned, but it is not yet known whether it was poison or the blow to his head which killed him. The injury to the head would have caused death instantly, had he still been alive when he was hit. It has now been discovered that Ms Brown, the chief suspect, was with friends five miles away from the murder scene between 7 pm and 10 pm on Saturday.

Answers to Exercise 14 are given on p. 151.

Exercise 15: Assessing implications

For each of the following passages, assume that what is said in the passage is true, and assess whether each of the responses (a) to (e) is *true, false, probably true, probably false,* or whether you have *insufficient information* in the passage to draw any conclusion about the statement's truth or falsity. Write your answer – *T, F, PT, PF,* or *II* – at the end of each of the sentences (a) to (e). You may find it interesting to compare your answers to the exercise with someone else's.

1 A study from Sweden reports that the incidence of skin cancer increased by 50 per cent between 1979 and 1987. Exposure to sunlight is known to cause skin cancer in light-skinned people. The incidence of skin cancer was found to be higher amongst professionals than amongst manual workers – thus it was higher amongst those who can afford to take holidays in places with very sunny climates. Twenty per cent of skin cancer cases occurred amongst those aged between 20 and 39, although most types of cancer are uncommon in this age group.

(Report in the Independent, *30 March, 1993)*

(a) Manual workers in Sweden have no risk of getting skin cancer.
(b) There is a lower risk of skin cancer for those aged over forty than for those aged under forty.
(c) The increase in the incidence of skin cancer in Sweden indicates that exposure to sunlight cannot be the only cause of skin cancer.
(d) Those aged over 40 in Sweden are more likely than the rest of the population to take holidays in places with sunny climates.
(e) The increased incidence of skin cancer in Sweden may be due to an increase in the numbers of people taking holidays in places with sunny climates.

2 Nearly 600 people, most of whom had an inflated sense of their own safety as car drivers, took part in a study which investigated ways of getting people to drive more safely. The drivers were asked to fill in a questionnaire detailing an imaginary accident which they had caused and which had serious repercussions, such as the loss of a child's life. They had to write a description of the consequences, and imagine the subsequent guilt, lack of confidence or inability to drive again. Before the study, 50 per cent of the group said they would be prepared to drive at over 80 miles per hour on a motorway. After completion of the questionnaire, this figure fell to 27 per cent. The group most likely to overestimate their driving skills and safety were young men.

(Report in the Independent, *5 November 1993)*

(a) Most drivers have an inflated sense of their own safety.
(b) Some drivers who overestimate their driving skills tend to drive too fast.

(c) People with only a few years' driving experience do not overestimate their skills.
(d) Forcing drivers to imagine that they have had a serious road accident may make them drive more responsibly in the future.
(e) Imagining that one has caused a serious accident has the undesirable effect of reducing one's confidence as a driver.

3 Many people who have bad headaches worry that this might be the first symptom of a brain tumour. Such worries are almost always groundless. Neurologists are agreed that a headache which has persisted for a year with no other symptoms is unlikely to be due to a brain tumour. The early symptoms of brain tumours are indeed headaches which are worst on waking, accompanied by vomiting, failing vision and, later, drowsiness. If there is a tumour at the front of the skull, the first symptom may be a change in personality. All of these symptoms, however, have other possible causes. It is possible to diagnose tumours with brain scanning techniques, and early diagnosis improves the chances of successful treatment.

(Independent on Sunday, *21 March 1993)*

(a) A change in someone's personality indicates that they have a brain tumour.
(b) Brain scanning can be carried out without risk of harm to the patient.
(c) Neurologists think that headaches are never symptoms of brain tumour.
(d) People suffering from headaches, vomiting and failing vision would be wise to have a brain scan.
(e) Someone suffering from headaches, vomiting and failing vision is not necessarily suffering from a brain tumour.

4 A technique for inducing phantom sheep pregnancies has been developed to address the problem of what to do with the million lambs born each year to mothers which for one reason or another cannot breast-feed them. Fostering is notoriously difficult because a ewe quickly forms a bond with its own lamb and rejects all others. Farmers are forced to rear orphaned lambs themselves, and lack of maternal contact can cause behaviour abnormalities. Gently stretching the neck of the cervix with two fingers sends nerve signals to the animal's brain that mimic those produced in labour. The sheep believes it has given birth to a second lamb. The orphaned lamb can then be introduced to its new mother with an 80 per cent chance that it will be accepted.

(Independent, *22 March 1993)*

(a) A ewe which gives birth to two lambs from one pregnancy will form bonds with both lambs.
(b) A ewe will actually reject her own lamb if she is introduced to an orphaned lamb.

(c) An orphaned lamb may fail to develop normal behaviour if it is not fostered by a ewe.
(d) An orphaned lamb needs maternal contact in order to grow to adulthood.
(e) The formation of a bond between a ewe and a lamb can occur even if the ewe is not the mother of the lamb.

5 Dipping of sheep protects the animals from scab and blowfly attacks. Leather manufacturers report that since sheep dipping ceased to be compulsory last year, 60 per cent of British sheepskins have been found to have damage from these parasites. But there are worries that sheep dips can cause health problems for farmers who use them. The Veterinary Products Committee examined medical evidence on 266 cases of people who believed that their influenza-like symptoms were caused by exposure to sheep dip. They found a possible link to sheep dip in only 58 of these cases, and of these 58, only three had worn protective clothing while using the dip. The long-term effects of low level exposure to sheep dip are not known. However, because of concerns about safety, the Ministry of Agriculture has introduced legislation requiring farmers who use sheep dips to have a certificate of competence.

(Independent, 2 December 1993)

(a) Scab and blowfly cause distress to sheep.
(b) There is no evidence that there may be a link between influenza-like symptoms and the use of sheep dips.
(c) Protective clothing prevents sheep dip from damaging farmers' health.
(d) Low-level exposure to sheep dip is known to be dangerous enough to justify banning the use of the dip.
(e) Sheep dips need to be handled with great care because they present a risk to the health of farmers who use them.

Answers to Exercise 15 are given on p. 151.

Recognizing implications of arguments

Sometimes a whole argument has implications which go beyond the particular subject with which it is concerned. There are two important ways in which an argument can do this – by exhibiting a particular structure or shape, which it can have in common with arguments on other topics, or by relying on a general principle which can be applied to other cases. The skills involved in dealing with implications of arguments can be described as *recognizing parallel arguments* and *recognizing and applying principles*.

Recognizing parallel arguments

The value of this skill is that being able to recognize parallel arguments may help us to see what is wrong with an argument. Sometimes it is easier for us to recognize a flaw in an argument if the argument is about a familiar subject. Suppose you are presented with an argument on an unfamiliar topic, and although you doubt your ability to assess the subject matter, you can nevertheless see that the argument has a particular shape or pattern. If you can substitute some familiar subject matter into this pattern, you may be able to see whether the argument is good. Not all arguments can be dealt with in this way; those which can, tend to be relatively short and to succeed or fail in virtue of their structure, rather than because there is additional evidence which counts against them.

Someone who objects to an argument by saying 'You might as well argue that . . . ' is often presenting a parallel argument to show that there is a problem with the original argument. This is what is happening in the two following examples of conversations:

1 *James:* I mean what I say because I say what I mean.
John: You might as well argue that you eat what you see because you see what you eat.

2 *Sam:* We have all had the experience of being deceived by our senses – the stick which looks bent when it is straight, and so on – and all the information we get through our senses in this way is potentially illusory, therefore sense experience is always unreliable.
Jo: You might as well argue that since we've all had the experience of being lied to – that even lovers lie and that everyone is potentially untrustworthy, therefore no-one can ever be trusted.

The argument presented in Exercise 5 (p. 22) offers an example in which, if we construct a parallel argument, we can see that an unwarranted inference has been made. The argument concerned the claim that there is no justification for public discussion and condemnation of the sex life of the US president. In order to persuade us that a husband who deceives his wife can nevertheless be a good president, it gave examples of presidents who had been good husbands (in the sense that they did not deceive their wives) but bad presidents. We could summarize this section of the argument as follows:

Someone who does not deceive his wife can nevertheless be a bad president.
So someone who does deceive his wife can be a good president.

Although the conclusion here may be true, and although – especially if we agree with the conclusion – we may be tempted to think that a good reason has been offered for it, in fact the first sentence is not a good reason for accepting the conclusion.

This is evident if we look at the following parallel argument:

> Someone who is not cruel to children can nevertheless be a bad child-minder. So someone who is cruel to children can be a good child-minder.

We can immediately see with this example that the conclusion cannot be true, because someone who is cruel to children cannot possibly be a good child-minder. If the conclusion must be false, then this cannot be a good argument even if the reason offered is true. The reason no doubt is true, because in order to be a good child-minder you have to do more than merely refrain from cruelty to children. The argument is bad because the reason is not sufficient to establish the conclusion, and if this is so with the argument about child-minders, then it is also the case with the parallel argument about US presidents. Whether or not a president who deceives his wife can nevertheless be a good president depends upon whether the tendency to deceive extends to all areas of the president's life. It does not depend upon whether a president who is an exemplary husband deceives the public about some of his actions.

Exercise 16: Identifying parallel arguments

In these multiple-choice questions, you should pick the answer which uses reasoning parallel to the reasoning in the original passage.

1 Because heroin addicts usually have one or more needle marks on their arms, and Robert has some needle marks on his arm, it follows that Robert is probably a heroin addict.

Which of the following most closely parallels the reasoning used in the argument above?

(a) Because patients with malaria usually have high fevers, and George is a patient with malaria, George probably has a high fever.
(b) Because patients with malaria usually have high fevers, malaria probably causes high fevers.
(c) Because doctors have high incomes, and people with high incomes pay high taxes, doctors probably pay high taxes.
(d) Because students are usually under twenty-five years old, and Harold is under twenty-five years old, Harold is probably a student.
(e) Because heroin addicts usually have needle marks on their arms, most heroin addicts probably inject the drug directly into their veins.

(Law School Admission Test, Feb. 1986)

2 It has usually been claimed that in eras of high infant mortality, parents adopted indifference to children as an emotional defence. But some scholars deny that parents were indifferent to children because so many

died, arguing instead that children died because their parents were so unconcerned about them as to spare no time for them.

Which of the following is most similar in its structure to the argument described in the last sentence above?

(a) It was not the school's new reading programme, but parents' increased concern with their children's schoolwork that produced better reading scores.
(b) It is not true that the lack of qualified workers depresses wages in the poor sectors of an industrial economy; rather, the low wages attract unskilled labour.
(c) It is not changing demand that prompts the introduction of new fashions; actually the clothing industry brings in new fashions whether the public wants them or not.
(d) It is not true that those who take illegal drugs harm only themselves; by supporting organized crime, they harm society as well.
(e) It was not considered worthy of a poet to write for the Elizabethan theatre; nevertheless, many poets did so.

(Law School Admission Test, June 1983)

3 The achievement of zero population growth in Great Britain has not forestalled the recent political and economic decline of Great Britain. We must conclude that rapid population growth is not the economic disaster social scientists have led us to believe it to be.

Which of the following is most like the argument above?

(a) Many people who do not smoke cigarettes develop chronic respiratory illnesses; therefore, cigarette smoking cannot be the health risk it is supposed to be.
(b) Jerry bought expensive paint but she still had to apply two coats to the wall to cover the old colour; therefore, you might as well buy the cheapest paint available.
(c) Even if the country uses less energy this year than it did last year, more oil will be imported than was imported last year; therefore, energy conservation should be encouraged.
(d) This drug causes certain side effects in a small percentage of the population; we can conclude that it is safe for the majority of people.
(e) Some of his paintings are dull and uninspired; we can conclude that he is not in the same class as the greatest artists.

(Law School Admission Test, Sept. 1984)

Answers to Exercise 16 are given on p. 154.

Recognizing and applying principles

Arguments which rely on general principles have implications beyond their own subject matter, because it is in the nature of a general principle that it is applicable to more than one case. A piece of reasoning may use such a principle without explicitly describing it as a general principle, so we need to be alert to the fact that some of the statements in an argument may apply to cases other than the one under discussion. There can be many kinds of principle, for example, legal rules, moral guidelines, business practices, and so on. Principles may function in an argument as reasons, as conclusions or as unstated assumptions. So, when we are going through the usual process of identifying reasons, conclusions and assumptions, we should ask ourselves whether any of them is a statement with general applicability.

The skill of identifying principles is valuable, because sometimes the application of a principle to other cases – that is to say, the further implications of a principle – may show us that the principle needs to be modified, or maybe even rejected. Suppose, for example, someone wants to argue against the use of capital punishment, and offers as a reason 'Killing is wrong'. This principle, stated as it is without any qualification, obviously has very wide applicability. It applies to all cases of killing. So, if we are to accept it as a principle to guide our actions, it means that killing in wartime is wrong, and killing in self-defence is wrong. If we are convinced that killing in self-defence cannot be wrong, then we have to modify our original principle in order to take account of exceptions to it. Applying principles involves being consistent in our reasoning, recognizing all the implications of our own and others' reasoning.

Another example is offered by a debate in the sphere of medical ethics. It has been suggested that when the demand for treatment for illness exceeds the resources available, and thus decisions have to be made about priorities, one type of illness which should come very low on the list of priorities for treatment is illness which individuals bring upon themselves by their actions or lifestyles. Such illness can be described as 'self-inflicted'. Most doctors would *not* take the view that self-inflicted illness should not be treated, but it is an issue which is often mentioned when public opinion is consulted about how best to use the resources available for health care. For example, someone may say, 'We should not give high priority to expensive heart treatments for smokers, because they have brought their illness on themselves.'

Clearly the principle underlying this is that 'We should not give high priority to the treatment of self-inflicted illness', and it is a principle with wider applicability. But in order to understand to which cases of illness it properly applies, we need to be clearer about what exactly is meant by 'self-inflicted illness'. At the very least it must mean an illness which has been caused by the actions or behaviour of the person who is ill. On this definition, the principle would apply to a very wide range of illnesses – for example, smoking related diseases, alcohol and drug related diseases, diseases caused by unsuitable diet, some sports injuries, some road accident injuries, some cases of sexually transmitted disease. However, it may be claimed that one cannot properly be said to have *inflicted* a disease on oneself unless one *knew* that the action or behaviour would cause the illness, or it may be claimed that a disease cannot properly be said to be *self*-inflicted, if the action which caused the disease was carried out under some kind of compulsion or addiction.

So, perhaps one would wish to modify the definition of 'self-inflicted illness' to read, 'an illness which has knowingly been caused by the deliberate and free action of an individual'. This definition would give the principle narrower applicability. For example, it would not be applicable to diseases caused by bad diet when the individual did not know the effects of a bad diet. Nor would it apply to cases of illness caused by addiction. But we may still find that those cases to which it did apply – for example, a motor-cyclist injured in a road accident through not wearing a crash helmet – suggested to us that there was something wrong with the principle.

Exercise 17: Applying and evaluating principles

For each of the following principles, think of a case to which it applies, and consider whether this particular application suggests to you that the principle should be modified or abandoned. This exercise would work well as the basis for a class discussion.

1 No-one should have to subsidize, through taxation, services which they themselves never use.

2 We should not have laws to prevent people from harming themselves, provided their actions do not harm others.

3 There should be absolute freedom for the newspapers to publish anything they wish.

4 Doctors should be completely honest with their patients.

5 You should never pass on information which you have promised to keep secret.

Answers to Exercise 17 are given on p. 156.

Chapter 4

Two skills in the use of language

Our earlier discussions of examples have relied upon the exercise of a skill which has not yet been explicitly mentioned – the understanding of language. This, of course, lies behind anyone's ability in critical thinking, since to think critically essentially involves dealing with reasoning which is expressed in language. Different individuals have differing levels of skill in dealing with language, but this is another skill which can improve with practice. You can extend your vocabulary, and increase your ability to deal with complex sentence structure. No specific exercises are offered in this book to practise these abilities, but this chapter will deal with two skills in language use which are directly related to reasoning well – the ability to use language with clarity and precision, and the ability to summarize someone else's reasoning.

The first of these skills is one which a good reasoner will have to possess, because sometimes the evaluation of reasoning crucially depends upon the clarification of the exact meaning of a word or phrase. The second skill – being able to summarize reasoning – is concerned primarily with understanding, rather than evaluating, reasoning. But since evaluation is not possible without understanding, and since summarizing is a useful aid to understanding, the development of this skill will be of great value.

Using language with clarity and precision

It is in the nature of the English language that words can have more than one meaning, and thus that sometimes the use of a word, or of a phrase, can be ambiguous. One trick upon which people sometimes rely when presenting an argument is to use an ambiguous word deliberately in order to lead people to accept a conclusion which the reasoning offered does not entitle them to draw. What is supposed to be a classic example of this trick appears in the following extract from *Utilitarianism* by John Stuart Mill:

> The only proof capable of being given that an object is visible is that people actually see it. The only proof that a sound is audible is that people hear it: and so of the other sources of experience. In like manner, I apprehend, the sole evidence it is possible to produce that anything is desirable, is that people do actually desire it.
>
> *(J.S. Mill,* Utilitarianism, *Collins/Fontana, p. 288)*

The ambiguous word here is 'desirable', and critics of Mill claim that in this passage, given the comparison of 'desirable' with 'visible' and 'audible', the meaning of 'desirable' must be 'can be desired'. Yet, they say, Mill goes on to use this passage as a basis for the claim that happiness is 'desirable' in the sense that it 'ought to be desired'. In order to assess whether Mill really is attempting to play this trick, you would need to read Chapter 4 of *Utilitarianism*, where you may find more clues in the text as to the exact meaning which Mill intended. But for our purposes the example serves to illustrate the way in which a word may be used ambiguously.

Not all cases of ambiguity are deliberate. We looked at the following argument in Chapter 2:

> If cigarette advertising were banned, cigarette manufacturers would save the money they would otherwise have spent on advertising. Thus, in order to compete with each other, they would reduce the price of cigarettes. So, banning cigarette advertising would be likely to lead to an increase in smoking.

We noted that it was not clear whether the phrase 'an increase in smoking' meant that the numbers of people who smoke would increase, or that those who smoke would smoke more, or both. There is no particular reason to think that this phrase has been left unclear deliberately in order to persuade us to accept an otherwise ill-founded conclusion. In this short passage, there are no further clues as to what the author might have meant. The person presenting the argument may have had a very clear idea of what they meant by the phrase, and may have believed that the argument gave strong support to the conclusion. Perhaps the exact meaning of the phrase was not spelt out because the author did not notice the ambiguity.

In such cases we need to evaluate both possible interpretations. Would a reduction in the price of cigarettes be likely to persuade more people to smoke? This is questionable, since it seems unlikely that what deters people from smoking is the price of cigarettes. Amongst those who do not smoke, there are, presumably, some who have never wanted to do so, and some who have given up smoking solely because of the health risks. For people in these two categories, the cost of cigarettes plays no part in their motivations. It is just possible – but very unlikely – that some ex-smokers would return to smoking, if only cigarettes were cheaper. It is possible, and a little more likely, that some non-smokers – perhaps young people who have not yet developed the habit – would become smokers if cigarettes were cheaper.

Let us turn to the other interpretation – would a reduction in the price of cigarettes be likely to result in smokers smoking more? This is possible. There may be some smokers who restrict the number of cigarettes they smoke per day because they are expensive, who would like to smoke more, and who think that a few more cigarettes per day would not increase the health risks which they already incur.

We have seen two examples where an ambiguous word or phrase is used. In such cases, we need to look for clues in the text as to which interpretation is intended. If we are unable to find such clues, we need to evaluate the reasoning in relation to each of the possible interpretations.

Another type of case in which clarification is required is where a term is used which is obviously intended to encompass a whole class of objects, but since the writer's meaning has not been made clear, it is not immediately apparent what exactly the term covers. An example was presented in the last chapter, under the discussion of the application of principles. The principle in question was 'We should not give high priority to the treatment of self-inflicted illness'. It would not be possible to evaluate reasoning which relied on this principle until we had clarified the exact definition of the term 'self-inflicted illness'. Sometimes in such cases there will be clues in the text as to what the author must mean. Where we can find no such clues, we must consider all the definitions which we think are possible, and assess the reasoning based upon each of these in turn.

Exercise 18: Clarifying words or phrases

For each of the following passages, identify any word or phrase which is crucial to the reasoning, and which you think needs to be clarified. Identify the different possible interpretations of the word or phrase, and assess the difference they make to the reasoning in the passage.

1 What makes a beautiful face? How long or short should the perfect nose

be; is there an optimal length to the face or ear lobe; what should the angle of the eyes be in respect to the bridge of the nose? Recent research suggests that beauty is simply a matter of being Mr or Ms Average.

Three hundred psychology students were asked to rate pictures of faces using an attractiveness score of one to five. Some of the pictures were of a single individual, and some were composite faces, made up from the features of two, four, eight, sixteen or up to thirty-two individual faces. The lowest scores for attractiveness were those for individual faces. The attractiveness ratings increased with the number of faces used to make a composite face.

So, take heart! Beauty is only the sum total of our big and little noses, receding and protruding chins, high and low foreheads. In order to be beautiful you do not have to be unusual – you only have to be average after all.

2 It is important that in bringing up children we should try to develop in them the quality of empathy, because those who lack it can be dangerous. For example, child molesters and psychopaths are dangerous precisely because they do not care about the suffering of others. However, children will need more than the quality of empathy in order to grow up into the kind of citizens we want, because empathy can be used in good or evil ways – for example by the businessman who can use his understanding of others in order to inspire colleagues or in order to exploit them.

3 Doctors should always be honest with their patients. If a doctor tells a patient a lie, and they find out they have been deceived, then the relationship of trust which is crucial for successful medical treatment will have broken down. Moreover, since patients have a right to know everything about their medical condition, those patients who ask doctors about their condition should be given truthful answers to their questions.

Answers to Exercise 18 are given on p. 157.

Summarizing arguments

For most of the examples in this book, we have set out the structure of arguments simply by using the exact wording of the passages under consideration. In doing so, we have picked out the relevant parts of a passage – basic reasons and intermediate conclusions (both stated and unstated), and main conclusions – and set them out in a way which shows the progression of the reasoning. This may be quite easy to do with short passages, especially if they have very clear conclusion indicators and reason indicators. But with longer pieces, such as are often found in newspapers, you need a clear understanding of the whole passage before you can attempt to set out all the steps in the reasoning. Writing a summary can help with this understanding in two ways. First, having to express something in your own words forces you to come to grips with exactly what the passage is saying. Secondly, the particular kind of summary recommended here helps you to make a long argument more manageable by breaking it down into smaller stages.

First, pick out the main conclusion, either by identifying conclusion indicators, or by asking 'What is the main message which this passage is trying to get me to believe or accept?' Then pick out the *immediate* reasons which are intended to support this. These could be basic reasons and/or intermediate conclusions. Don't try to summarize all the reasoning at this stage – for example, do not try to work out exactly how the intermediate conclusions (if any) are supported. Just concentrate on the one or two (or three, or more) statements immediately supporting the main conclusion. Then express the main conclusion and the statements supporting it in your own words. Your summary could have the following form:

> The passage is trying to get me to accept that . . . [main conclusion] . . . , on the grounds that . . . [intermediate conclusion 1] . . . and . . . [basic reason] . . . and . . . [intermediate conclusion 2].

When you have written this first brief summary, you will have a framework into which you can fit the more detailed reasoning. You can then take each intermediate conclusion in turn, and ask what reasons are offered in support of it. Let's apply this to an example.

Example 1: Nicotine for smokers

> Nicotine products, such as nicotine gum and nicotine patches, should be made available cheaply, widely advertised, and given endorsement from health authorities. This would make it likely that smokers would transfer their addiction to these less harmful products.
>
> It is the impurities in tobacco which cause cancer, accounting for one third of cancer deaths in Britain per year, whereas the nicotine in tobacco provides pleasure, stimulation and stress relief. Although the impurities in tobacco could be removed, it is unlikely that the tobacco industry will clean up its product as long as sales of tobacco are buoyant.
>
> It is thought that nicotine may be a contributory cause of heart disease. But the benefits to health from giving up tobacco are likely to outweigh the risks of taking nicotine.

What is the main message which this passage is trying to get us to accept? It is clearly concerned with the idea that nicotine products should be promoted, as a means of trying to get smokers to stop smoking tobacco.

The immediate reason it gives for promoting nicotine is that doing so would make it more likely that smokers would switch from harmful tobacco to less harmful nicotine products. So our first attempt at a summary would be:

> The passage is trying to get me to accept that nicotine products should be made available cheaply, widely advertised, and given endorsement from health authorities, on the grounds that these products are less harmful than tobacco, and that promoting them would make it likely that smokers would stop smoking and use these products instead.

We have extracted two reasons here from the second sentence – that the products are less harmful than tobacco, and that promoting them would change smokers' behaviour. The rest of the passage is principally concerned with giving support to the first of these reasons – trying to show that these products *are* less harmful than tobacco. But paragraphs two and three can also be seen as lending some support to an unstated intermediate conclusion that if smokers knew more about which components of tobacco give them pleasure, and which put them at risk of cancer, they would switch to using nicotine products other than tobacco, especially if nicotine patches and gum were relatively cheap.

Example 2: Subsidizing the arts

Now let's try summarizing a longer passage:

> [Some people maintain that there is no case for subsidising the arts because they are a minority interest.] In its most sympathetic – or least unattractive – guise, this view presents itself as defending the interest of the poor. What subsidy for the arts amounts to is taking money from all the taxpayers (including those who never set foot in a museum or theatre, let alone the Royal Opera House) to help pay for the leisure activities of the privileged classes. And why, they say, should we subsidise snobbish entertainments such as opera when we don't subsidise proletarian ones such as football?
>
> Quite apart from the patronising assumption that most ordinary people are permanently immune to culture, however inexpensive it might be made by subsidy (free in the case of most museums), there is an odd anomaly in this argument. Taken to its logical conclusion, it would undermine any kind of taxation in a democratic society. What is the difference between claiming that people should not have to pay for the arts if they never use them and saying that they should not have to support the school system if they are childless, or pay for road building if they have no car?
>
> The way we collect and spend taxes is not based on the same principle as paying for private services. If the country decides that it believes certain things, whether universal schooling or the preservation of its cultural heritage, to be for the good of the nation as a whole, it does not require that every single taxpayer partake of those good things.

> So why is art a good thing? Why is it so important that Covent Garden be given millions of pounds of our money, even though so few of us go to the opera, when thousands of people who prefer to play golf have to pay for it themselves? Why should my pastime be more worthy than yours?
>
> John Stuart Mill was compelled to modify the simplistic utilitarian principle that good consisted in 'the greatest happiness of the greatest number', because it implied that all pleasures were equal: that pushpin was as good as poetry. The arts are not just an eccentric hobby. What the arts offer us is a way both of making sense of our condition and of transcending it. They are, in the end, what makes us human rather than bestial.
>
> *(Janet Daley, Copyright ©* The Times, *12 October 1995)*

What is this passage trying to get us to accept? It discusses one type of argument against subsidizing the arts from public money, and says that 'there is an odd anomaly in this argument'. It also seeks to explain why art is a good thing – the kind of thing which can be judged to be for the good of the nation as a whole. So clearly it is trying to convince us that one argument against subsidizing the arts is a bad argument, and that there is a positive reason for subsidizing the arts. Our first summary could be as follows:

> The passage is trying to get me to accept that subsidizing the arts is a good thing, on the grounds that, like universal schooling, the arts are good for the nation as a whole, and things which are good for the nation as a whole should be subsidized from public money, even though some people who pay taxes may never use these services.

Two immediate reasons have been identified here – that the arts are good for the nation, and that it is appropriate to subsidize things which are good for the nation even if some taxpayers do not use them.

The first of these reasons is given support by the claim that the arts 'are, in the end, what makes us human rather than bestial'. The second reason is supported by showing the implications of the principle sometimes used to defend the claim that we should *not* subsidize the arts – that principle being, that we should not subsidize from taxes those services which some taxpayers do not use. This would mean that taxes should not be used to subsidize education and road building because some taxpayers don't have children, and some don't drive cars. Since (it is assumed) these implications are unacceptable, the principle from which they follow should be rejected, and we should accept instead the principle that things which are good for the nation as a whole should be subsidized from tax revenue.

In these two examples, we have offered an initial simple summary, which does not seek to set out all the steps of the argument, but aims to identify the principal reasons which give immediate support to the main conclusion. We have then shown how, with this first brief summary as a basis, we can fill in the reasoning in a more detailed way. Exercise 19 gives you a chance to practise doing this.

In some particularly long or complex passages (for example, some of those in Exercise 20 – especially 6, 7, 9 and 10), you may find it helpful to look first for themes in different sections of the passage, and to summarize each theme before you try to summarize the main conclusion and reasons.

Exercise 19: Writing a summary

For each of the following passages:

- Write a summary of the main conclusion and the immediate reasons (basic reasons or intermediate conclusions) offered for it,
- Identify the reasoning which is meant to support any intermediate conclusion you have identified.

1 It has been suggested that more generous damages for the victims of medical negligence would only serve to increase the number of doctors practising defensive medicine – treatment tailored not to the need of the patient, but to the doctor's desire to avoid litigation.

The test of whether there has been any negligence in medical negligence actions is whether the doctor has departed from the standard of a reasonably competent doctor – a standard that in practice is set by the medical profession, not the courts. It is therefore difficult to see how a 'doctor's desire to avoid litigation' can be satisfied by adopting treatment that is not tailored to the need of the patient, because the need of the patient is precisely what the reasonably competent doctor should have in mind when making a diagnosis or giving treatment. On the contrary, the more that the doctor thinks about the courts rather than the interests of the patient, the more likely it is that she will find herself on the wrong end of a writ for negligence.

Nor is it clear how higher levels of compensation will produce this defensive reaction in doctors, since doctors do not themselves pay the compensation. The vast majority of medical accidents occur in hospitals. Since January 1990 the payment of damages for the consequences of negligence in NHS hospitals has been the responsibility of the health authorities.

If a 'defensive' state of mind, which is sometimes confused with 'defensive medicine' makes the doctor more careful, this may be to the benefit of both patients and doctors if it results in the prevention of avoidable errors.

(Letter to the Editor, Independent, *21 September 1993)*

2 The results of IQ tests taken at an early age cannot be used to indicate future success in life. For the greatest reliability, information on any human

abilities should be collected at different points in an individual's life. Many outstanding people such as Freud and Einstein were not seen as highly intelligent even by the age of twenty, and certainly not by the age of ten. Picasso always had difficulty with reading because he had very little schooling, and so would have scored a very low IQ. The tests are not even a sensitive measure of exceptionally high intelligence, because of the 'ceiling effect', the upper limit of the tests being too low to distinguish between the top few per cent.

All long-term follow-up studies using an IQ measure show that, in whatever ways intelligence is defined and measured, it is only part of the complex causation of success, which must include opportunity and the will to strive. For example, the latest results from the Terman studies on gifted children in California, which have been going on since the Twenties, has found that, regardless of the IQ scores, the subjects were not noticeably more successful in adulthood than if they had been randomly selected from the same social and economic backgrounds.

The big influences in determining future achievement are socioeconomic status and gender. In the Far East, though, success is attributed to hard work rather than any IQ score, which probably explains why in America many young Asians with lower IQs are more successful than others of higher measured intelligence.

(Letter to the Editor, Independent, *28 June 1995)*

3 In many parts of the world, young girls who become pregnant under the age of 16 face a real risk of death; in Africa the maternal mortality rate in girls aged 10-14 is five times higher than in women aged 20. The main hazard for the very young mother is that her pelvis will not have finished growing and will not be big enough for the baby to pass through. If the baby is too large for the pelvis the mother has to hope she will be able to be delivered using forceps or by caesarean section. Without skilled obstetric care, she will face a long, obstructed labour likely to end with a dead baby and damage to her pelvic organs – even if she escapes with her life.

The teenage mother in the West is likely to be better nourished and physically more mature than her counterpart in developing countries, but prospects for her baby are still worse than for the baby of an older woman. Babies born to teenagers are smaller, more likely to be premature and more likely to die during the first year of life. Until recently the assumption was that these risks were linked to the social deprivation of many teenage mothers, who are more likely than the rest of the population to be unmarried and less well educated. Yet research in Utah shows that white, married women in their teens who receive quality care during their pregnancies have poorer outcomes than older women. Their babies are twice as likely to be premature and undersized. The increased risk for mothers under 20 continues into the next pregnancy; a second baby born to a teenager is also more likely to be underweight or premature. The explanation for the higher risk of complications in teenage pregnancy in the West is likely to be similar to that in developing countries: a teenager hasn't finished growing. This may lead to both mother and infant competing for nutrients, while the immature uterus may predispose the mother to infective and other complications.

Some politicians may use these statistics to denigrate teenage mothers. But the message we should draw is that the next generation of children will be healthier if mothers can choose not to become pregnant until they are mature. That means providing teenagers with the sex education and contraception they need to take control of their reproductive health.

(Dr Tony Smith, Independent on Sunday, *9 July 1995)*

Answers to Exercise 19 are given on p. 158.

Chapter 5

Exercising the skills of reasoning

Most of the reasoning which you will encounter and want to assess – in, for example, newspapers, journals and textbooks – will not be presented in neat, short passages typical of the majority of those in this book. Instead, you will often find that you have to extract the reasoning from a long passage which may contain some irrelevant material, and which may present reasons and conclusions in a jumbled way, rather than setting them out in what would seem to be a clear series of steps. The task of assessing a long passage also differs from most of the exercises in this book, in that, rather than focusing on one particular skill, it requires you to bring all your reasoning skills into play. You will have to play the whole game, choosing the appropriate skills, just as the tennis player has to play a game, choosing whether their well practised forehand drive or their beautifully honed backhand volley is the appropriate shot.

You have already had the opportunity to practise your skills on some longer passages in Exercise 13 (p. 61). In this chapter, we shall show some examples of analysis and evaluation of long passages of reasoning, and end with some passages with which you can get to grips yourself.

Longer passages of reasoning

Dealing with longer passages of reasoning can seem daunting at first, but it helps if we remember that the same skills are called for, whatever the length of the passage. We shall present the important steps, expanding on the list set out in Chapter 3:

1 The first task is to identify the conclusion and the reasons. You may find conclusion indicators (such as 'therefore' or 'so') and reason indicators (such as 'because' or 'since') to help you to do this. But some passages will contain no such words, and you will need to identify the conclusion by understanding the main message of the passage. So start by reading the whole passage, and asking yourself 'What is this passage trying to persuade me to accept or believe?' When you have answered this, ask 'What immediate reasons or evidence is it presenting in order to get me to believe this?' It may be helpful at this stage to write a brief summary, on the following lines:

   This passage is trying to get me to accept
   that . . .,
   on the grounds that,
   first . . . ,
   second . . . , and so on.

With very long passages, it may also be helpful to break the passage down into smaller sections, and look for themes in different parts of the text, before writing your summary.

2 When you have sorted out what reasons are being offered, you need to consider what assumptions are being made. These could be:

   - assumptions which function as support for basic reasons, or as unstated additional reasons, or as unstated intermediate conclusions,
   - assumptions about the meanings of words or phrases, so look for ambiguous words and terms which require more precise definition,
   - assumptions that one case or one situation is analogous to or comparable with another, so look to see if any comparisons are being made,
   - assumptions that a particular explanation of a piece of evidence is the only plausible explanation, so look out for explanations.

In identifying assumptions, you are reconstructing the background of a particular piece of reasoning.

3 Once you are clear about the reasoning and its background, you need to evaluate it. Consider how far you can go in assessing the truth of the reasons and the unstated assumptions. Think about how you would seek further information to enable you to assess the truth of reasons.

4 Does the reasoning rely on evidence from sources whose authority is questionable?
5 Do you yourself have any knowledge which strengthens or weakens the conclusion? Or can you think of anything which *may* be true and which would have a bearing on the conclusion? (Remember to subject your own 'knowledge' to the same standards of scrutiny as you apply to the claims made by other people!)
6 If you have identified any explanations in the passage, are they plausible, and are they the *only* plausible explanations of what is being explained?
7 If you have found comparisons in the text, are these comparisons appropriate – that is to say, are the two things which are being compared alike in all relevant respects?
8 From the information in the passage, can you draw any important conclusions not mentioned in the passage? Do any of these conclusions suggest that the reasoning in the passage is faulty?
9 Is the reasoning in the passage (or any part of the reasoning) similar to – or parallel with – reasoning which you know to be faulty?
10 Do any of the reasons or assumptions embody a general principle? If there is any such general principle, can you think of any applications of it which would suggest that there is something wrong with the principle?
11 If you believe that the conclusion is not well supported by the reasons and assumptions, can you state the way in which the move from reasons to conclusion is flawed? Your answers to questions 5 to 10 above may help you to do this.

This list is primarily applicable to passages which do contain a recognizable argument, with a main conclusion and with some reasons or evidence offered in support of it. It is, however, possible to find passages which contain reasoning, but do not come to a major conclusion. Perhaps they examine evidence from two opposing sides of an issue, and leave readers to draw their own conclusions. Or perhaps they are seeking to explain something, as did the passages in Exercise 12. Even for passages without a main conclusion you will find it useful to go through the steps listed above in attempting to evaluate the reasoning.

Two examples of evaluation of reasoning

Example 1: Science versus theology

In your dismally unctuous leading article (18 March) asking for a reconciliation between science and 'theology', you remark that 'people want to know as much as possible about their origins'. I certainly hope they do, but what on earth makes you think that 'theology' has anything useful to say on the subject? Science is responsible for the following knowledge about our origins.

We know approximately when the universe began and why it is largely hydrogen. We know why stars form, and what happens in their interiors to convert hydrogen to other elements and hence give birth to chemistry in a world of physics. We know the fundamental principles of how a world of chemistry can become biology through the arising of self-replicating molecules. We know how the principle of self-replication gives rise, through Darwinian selection, to all life including humans.

It is science, and science alone, that has given us this knowledge and given it, moreover, in fascinating, overwhelming, mutually confirming detail. On every one of these questions theology has held a view that has been conclusively proved wrong. Science has eradicated smallpox, can immunize against most previous deadly viruses, can kill most previously deadly bacteria.

Theology has done nothing but talk of pestilence as the wages of sin. Science can predict when a particular comet will reappear and, to the second, when the next eclipse will occur. Science has put men on the moon and hurtled reconnaissance rockets around Saturn and Jupiter. Science can tell you the age of a particular fossil and that the Turin Shroud is a medieval fake. Science knows the precise DNA instructions of several viruses and will, in the lifetime of many present readers of the *Independent*, do the same for the human genome.

What has 'theology' ever said that is of the smallest use to anybody? When has 'theology' ever said anything that is demonstrably true and is not obvious? I have listened to theologians, read them, debated against them. I have never heard any of them ever say anything of the smallest use, anything that was not either platitudinously obvious or downright false.

If all the achievements of scientists were wiped out tomorrow there would be no doctors but witch-doctors, no transport faster than a horse, no computers, no printed books, no agriculture beyond subsistence peasant farming. If all the achievements of theologians were wiped out tomorrow, would anyone notice the smallest difference?

Even the bad achievements of scientists, the bombs and sonar-guided whaling vessels, *work*! The achievements of theologians don't do anything, don't affect anything, don't achieve anything, don't even mean anything. What makes you think that 'theology' is a subject at all?

(Letter to the Editor from Dr Richard Dawkins, Independent, *20 March 1993)*

Let us evaluate Dr Dawkins' argument, using the 11 steps listed earlier (pp. 88–89):

1 We must first try to write a brief summary of the passage, setting out what it seeks to persuade us to accept, and the reasons it gives why we should accept it. We are clearly being led to believe that theology is in some way inferior to science, because whereas science can give us a great deal of useful knowledge, theology cannot produce anything important or worthwhile. We could express the main theme as follows:

 This passage is trying to get me to accept that theology is not a respectable subject, in the way that science is, on the grounds that science has numerous achievements, all of which work, and most of which are beneficial, whereas the achievements of theology are ineffective and meaningless.

 We need to set out the reasons in a little more detail. What support is given for the idea that science is such a valuable activity? The passage mentions scientific knowledge about the origins of life and the universe, the success of science in eradicating illnesses, achievements in space exploration. It describes the restricted life we would have if the achievements of science were wiped out. It points out that even the bad achievements of science work.

 How does it seek to persuade us that theology is worthless? It claims that theology has been proved wrong about the origins of human life. It suggests that theology has contributed nothing to our understanding of the causes of disease – it 'has done nothing but talk of pestilence as the wages of sin'. It claims that theology has never said anything which is not either obvious or false. It suggests that no-one would notice if the achievements of theology were wiped out, and that these achievements, in contrast with even the bad achievements of science, do not work, have no effects, and have no meaning.

2 What assumptions underlie these reasons? The claim that science is responsible for 'knowledge' about our origins relies on the assumption that scientific theories – for example, theories about the origin of the universe, and the theory of evolution – constitute knowledge. Although the bad achievements of science are mentioned, they are not regarded as evidence that science is anything but a force for good, so there is an assumption that the bad effects of science do not outweigh the good effects. The conclusion that theology is not a subject relies upon an assumption that in order for something to be a subject, it must have some effect on people's lives, or some meaning for people's lives. Some of these assumptions may immediately strike you as questionable, but we shall deal with that presently under point 3.

Are there any words or phrases whose meaning needs to be clarified? There are some scientific terms – 'self-replicating molecules', 'DNA instructions', 'human genome'. We may not know the exact meanings of these terms, and perhaps this limits our ability to assess the claim that these aspects of scientific knowledge are worthwhile. If we do not know the context of this letter, we may question exactly what is meant by theology not being a *subject*. The letter was written in response to an article which welcomed the endowment of a lectureship in theology and natural science at Cambridge University, so Dawkins' view is that theology is not respectable as a subject of academic study.

Are any comparisons made? Yes, the whole passage is about the relative merits of science and theology. In concluding that theology does not qualify as a subject, the passage must assume that science and theology are comparable in at least one respect – in that both should measure up to certain standards in order to count as subjects of academic study.

Are there explanations which rely on assumptions? The second paragraph takes for granted that the scientific explanation of the origins of human beings – based on scientific theories – is the correct explanation.

3 To what extent can we assess the truth of the reasons and unstated assumptions? Even non-scientists will have no difficulty in accepting that scientific research is responsible for advances in medical knowledge, and, if technology is to be regarded as a part of science, for many of the things (transport, computers, books, modern agriculture) which make our lives easier and more enjoyable. Non-scientists may feel ill-qualified to judge whether theories about the origins of the universe and of human life have the status of knowledge, and also whether, for example, research into the DNA instructions of the human genome is valuable. We can all think of some of the bad effects of science – for example, weapons of mass destruction, pollution – and we can consider whether on balance science is a worthwhile activity.

What of the comments about the worthlessness of theology? Is it true that no-one would notice if the achievements of theologians were wiped out tomorrow? Is it true that theology achieves and means nothing? Surely this is something we can find out only by investigating the role which religion plays in people's lives. Maybe the thinking and the writings of theologians are of great value to many individuals, albeit in a very different way from the way in which science is valuable.

4 To what extent does the reasoning rely on authorities? The letter does not quote any specific sources, but the comments about the achievements of science derive their authority to some extent from the fact that the letter is written by a scientist. The whole area of scientific knowledge presents us with a dilemma in relation to the assessment of the reliability

of authorities. On the one hand, scientists are in a better position than non-scientists to assess the validity and, in some respects, the value of the results of scientific research. On the other hand, because their whole life's work may have been based on a particular theory, some scientists may not be in the best position to make unbiased judgements about evidence which goes against their views in a particular area of scientific knowledge. Moreover, in a discussion claiming that the whole activity of science is valuable, we would expect a scientist to emphasize those aspects favourable to the case, and perhaps play down the unfavourable aspects. Similarly we would expect a theologian to regard his or her own work as valuable. However, the case does not rest solely on Dawkins' authority as a scientist. We can all look at some of the effects of science, and consider whether the world is a better or a worse place for the existence of science.

5 What knowledge do you have which would strengthen or weaken the conclusion? We do know that science has some bad effects, and perhaps this weakens the case that we would be worse off without the achievements of science. Perhaps you know many people who find religion a great comfort in their lives, or who enjoy reading the works of theologians. This would weaken the claim that theology has no effect on anyone's lives. One could perhaps attempt to make a case for the superiority of theology over science, in that science has bad effects, whereas theology does not. However, some may point out the evil influences of some religious ideas – for example, intolerance and hostility to those who think differently. Dawkins does not take this line: in fact his claim that theology has no effects entails that it has no bad effects.

6 Is the scientific explanation of the origins of human beings more plausible than a theologian's explanation? Not all theologians will see a conflict between the two. Some Christians, for example, might say that the idea that human beings were created by God is compatible with the scientific explanation offered by the theory of evolution.

7 Does the text make any comparisons, and are they appropriate? We observed earlier that the passage assumes that in order to qualify as a 'subject', both science and theology must meet certain criteria and that theology fails to do so. One might see the text as implying that science makes an excellent job of what science is supposed to do – discovering information about the physical world, and usefully applying this information – whereas theology is hopeless at doing what science is supposed to do. But why should this disqualify it as a subject for academic study? When Dr Dawkins lists all the scientific questions on which theologians have held mistaken views, we might point out that so have scientists; and it is possible that our understanding of the world will be superseded in the future.

8 We have already mentioned two conclusions we can draw from the passage, one, that the bad effects of science *may* outweigh the good effects, and two, if theology has no effects, it has no bad effects.
9 One might be able to construct parallel reasoning, but nothing obvious springs to mind. However Dr Dawkins is judging theology in scientific terms, which may not be appropriate. We could show this by using a parallel question: What has science ever done to help us understand God?
10 We identified the general principle that for something to be an appropriate subject of study it must have some effect on people's lives, or some meaning for people's lives. This seems a reasonable principle, provided it is broadly interpreted so that history, for example, is regarded as having meaning for people's lives.
11 The main objections to the reasoning are that the comparison between science and theology is inappropriate, in that theology should not be required to be useful *in the same sphere* as science in order for it to be a proper subject for academic study; and that theology may well satisfy the principle which requires it to have some effect on – or some meaning for – people's lives.

Example 2: On the legalization of cannabis

This is not an ideal time to persuade politicians to talk about legalising drugs. Political parties are not in a mood to take risks. When they want to attract attention, they prefer to do so by offering thrusting new thoughts on the economy and other mainstream subjects. But crime is now as mainstream as you can get, and a great deal of crime is related to drugs. Any politician who talks about crime without confronting the debate on drugs is evading half the issue.

The recent police raid on 'Cannabis Café' in Brighton is only one example of police time being wasted on drug-related offences. How many houses were burgled and cars stolen in Brighton while the police were busy with the offending café? Yet the police were not to blame. The provocative opening of the café had been so well publicised that to have ignored it would have signalled that drug offences would now be ignored. The police are not entitled to convey such signals. They are supposed to uphold the law as it is, not as it should be.

What is wrong is the law itself. The criminalisation of cannabis derives from a number of prejudices and misconceptions. Although the drug is not entirely harmless, it is less harmful than tobacco. It is not addictive, nor dangerous in moderate quantities, and it does not provoke violent or anti-social behaviour. It mostly induces nothing worse that a state of rather happy, foolish withdrawal. It was partly this effect that worried orthodox society in the Sixties, because it became associated with the demotivation of an entire generation that was exaggeratedly seen as dropping out of the acquisitive, consumerist society. Cannabis was felt to be subversive.

Since then, successive generations have responded normally to economic stimuli and remained as acquisitive as anyone could wish. But they have continued to take cannabis. Almost all 25-year-olds in London have tried it, according to a recent survey by *Time Out* magazine. Cannabis should therefore have lost its association with drop-outs and have come to be seen as a recreational drug, offering much the same sort of respite from reality as alcohol but with less dangerous side-effects. It is also being found to have a widening variety of valuable medicinal qualities, particularly for the alleviation of multiple sclerosis.

In a period of rising crime, when practically every householder and car-owner feels vulnerable, and when peaceful citizens form vigilante groups because they are insufficiently protected by the proper authorities, it is absurd that the police and the courts should have had to spend valuable time dealing with 47,616 drug offences in 1991, and probably more last year, of which about 85 per cent concerned cannabis. Legalising the drug would save substantial amounts of time and money as well as bringing in tax revenue from legal sales. It would reduce the number of crimes committed to raise money for cannabis by lowering the price, unless heavily taxed, and undermine the power of the criminal underworld.

That world, however, is also deeply involved in hard drugs, which pose more complex problems since they can be dangerous and addictive. Some experts, including Commander John Grieve of the Metropolitan Police, believe the answer is to license and control the supply of all drugs. 'We need to undermine the economic or acquisitive base of drugs crime and the economic base of organised crime', he said at a conference in May.

If the Government wants to be seen to be serious about crime, it must look at the causes, one of which is drugs. A legal market in drugs under tight, selective controls, would not end drug-related crime, and people would still rob in order to raise money for drugs, but much more of the problem would be above ground and therefore more manageable. As suggested by Release, the drugs advisory service, this would be a suitable subject for a Royal Commission.

(Leading article, Independent*, 2 October 1993)*

1 What is this passage trying to persuade us to accept? The main message is that the law on cannabis should be changed. How could we best summarize the case which it makes out for this?

This passage is trying to get us to accept that the use of cannabis should be made legal, on the grounds that, first, cannabis is not very harmful; second, police time is wasted in investigating crimes involving cannabis; and third, fewer crimes of theft would occur if using cannabis were legal.

We need to look in more detail at these three lines of reasoning.

First, how is the claim that cannabis is not very harmful supported? In the third paragraph we are told that it is not addictive, not dangerous in moderate quantities, and does not provoke violent or anti-social behaviour, is less harmful than tobacco and, in the fourth paragraph, that it has less dangerous side-effects than alcohol. We are also told that its use does not turn people into drop-outs, the evidence offered for this being that almost all 25-year-olds in London have tried it, and they continue to conform to the acquisitive behaviour expected of members of the consumerist society. The medicinal value of cannabis is mentioned, particularly its use to alleviate multiple sclerosis.

The second line of reasoning concerns the waste of police time on drug offences, illustrated by the example of the police raid on the 'Cannabis Café'. In the fifth paragraph, figures are offered in support of the claim that the police spend valuable time dealing with drug offences, and especially those which concern the use of cannabis.

The fifth paragraph also contains the third major reason, that making cannabis legal would reduce crimes associated with the crime of using cannabis. It states that crimes are committed in order to raise money for buying cannabis, which could be cheaper if its use were legal. Another reason for legalizing cannabis is offered here, – that not only would it save money spent on police time, but it would also increase tax revenue from legal sales.

It is not clear what the final two paragraphs are meant to contribute to the reasoning, since they seem to change the subject. Instead of focusing on cannabis, they discuss what should be done about hard drugs, and suggest that a legal market in all drugs might lead to a reduction in crimes associated with drugs. We shall have to consider whether a strong enough case is made for the legalization of cannabis, bearing in mind that it may be weakened by these further comments about drugs in general.

2 What assumptions underlie the reasoning? The first line of reasoning makes comparisons between cannabis use and the use of tobacco and alcohol. It assumes that because we accept that the use of tobacco and alcohol should be legal, we should accept that the use of cannabis, which is claimed to be less harmful than either tobacco or alcohol, should also be legal. The facts that 'successive generations' have 'remained acquisitive' and 'almost all 25-year-olds in London have tried [cannabis]' are taken to indicate that taking cannabis is not associated with dropping out, but is merely done for recreational purposes. This seems to assume that the majority of 25-year-olds questioned in the survey have not tried cannabis just once or twice, but make a habit of using it.

The second line of reasoning refers to householders and car-owners feeling that they are insufficiently protected, whilst the police spend so much time on solving crimes concerning cannabis use. There is an assumption here that the time spent by the police on drug crimes reduces the time spent on other crimes. The third line of reasoning assumes that if cannabis use were legal, it would be taxed (hence increasing tax revenue), but not so highly that the price of cannabis would be the same as it is now (otherwise, the claim that legalization 'would reduce the number of crimes committed to raise money for cannabis' would not be supported).

There are no obviously ambiguous or insufficiently defined words, but it is not entirely clear what is being recommended in the final paragraph under the description – 'A legal market in drugs under tight, selective controls'. Does this mean that drugs would be available only on prescription, so that you could buy heroin, for example, but only if your doctor said you needed it for medical reasons? This interpretation suggests that the last two paragraphs do not have much to do with the argument about the legalization of cannabis, since what is being recommended in relation to cannabis seems to be that it should be legal to sell it as tobacco and alcohol are sold.

We have already mentioned the comparison with tobacco and alcohol, and there are no explanations of evidence (apart from the explanation of the evidence from the *Time Out* survey); indeed, no evidence is cited to show that cannabis is harmless, non-addictive, not dangerous and not anti-social.

3 We now need to assess the truth of the reasons and assumptions. We have to rely on the authority of medical evidence concerning the effects of cannabis, but we can attempt to read about a wide range of medical opinion. One problem with the absence of evidence that cannabis is harmful is that perhaps insufficient research has been done into its effects. The evidence as to how much police time is spent on offences concerning cannabis is presumably a statistic which could be checked, and police records would also, presumably, give some information about the number of thefts which are associated with cannabis use. Is cannabis really so expensive to buy that many people steal in order to buy it?

Now let us consider whether we should accept the assumptions. Should we accept that because the use of tobacco and alcohol is more harmful than cannabis, yet legal, the use of cannabis should also be legal? Why should we not conclude that the use of tobacco and alcohol should be made illegal? In order for this comparison to give support to the conclusion, more would need to be said about the undesirability of making tobacco and alcohol illegal.

The assumption about the results of the *Time Out* survey seems ill-founded. Even if all 25-year-olds in London have tried cannabis, we cannot assume that its recreational use is widespread amongst a group of 'normally' 'acquisitive' people, and hence that it is not associated with 'dropping out'. Moreover, if using cannabis is so common, can it be true that it is so expensive a habit that many people steal in order to buy cannabis?

The assumption that if the police spent less time on drug related crimes they would spend more time on crimes such as burglary and car theft is questionable. Perhaps they already do all that could reasonably be done about such crimes, short of having an unacceptably high level of police presence on the streets and police surveillance of everyone's lives and activities. However, even if the police were already doing all they could about burglaries and car crime, it might still be claimed to be a good thing to reduce the amount of time they spend on crime relating to cannabis, since this could reduce the costs of policing.

It seems reasonable to assume that the legal use of cannabis would be taxed, and that the taxes would not be set so high as to fail to reduce the incidence of theft to finance cannabis use.

4 Does the reasoning depend upon any unreliable sources? We have already pointed out that it relies on medical opinion, but there is no reason to think that doctors have a vested interest in making people believe that cannabis is relatively harmless. The passage refers to the opinion of Commander John Grieve of the Metropolitan Police that the supply of all drugs should be licensed and controlled. Is there any reason to regard this person as unreliable? It seems unlikely that he would make any personal gain from the legalization of drugs, but it is possible that his official role gives him a vested interest in reducing the amount of police time spent on drug offences.

5 Can we think of any additional information which would strengthen or weaken the conclusion? It is often claimed that using cannabis leads to the use of hard drugs, which are both dangerous and addictive, and that this is why the use of cannabis should be illegal. Suppose we found evidence to support the claim that many of those who use cannabis also go on to use hard drugs, would this weaken the conclusion? Perhaps not, because the temptation to go on to use hard drugs may exist only because cannabis use is illegal.

There is no reason to think that use of tobacco and alcohol lead to the use of hard drugs, so perhaps if cannabis had the same legal status as tobacco and alcohol, its use would have no connection with the use of hard drugs. Possibly this is something which could only be discovered from a trial period of legalization of cannabis. It is sometimes claimed that a tolerant attitude to the use of soft drugs in the Netherlands has led to an increase in drug-related crime and violence there. However, even if it is true that tolerance of the use of soft drugs has been a contributory cause of such problems (a claim which is disputed by the Dutch), there may be differences between Britain and the Netherlands such that the same result would not occur here.

6 We did not identify any explanations in the text.
7 We mentioned the comparison between cannabis on the one hand and alcohol and tobacco on the other. This is an appropriate comparison, since all are drugs, and their harmfulness should be the criterion which determines whether or not they ought to be legal. That means of course, that *all* their effects need to be taken into account, so if cannabis use would lead to hard drug use, whether it was legal or not, then perhaps it is harmful in a way in which tobacco and alcohol are not.
8 There are no obvious conclusions to draw from the passage, beyond those discussed in relation to assumptions.
9 No obvious parallel arguments come to mind.
10 We could perhaps regard the passage as relying on the principle that if something is not harmful, it should not be illegal. This seems a reasonable principle. What is at issue is whether cannabis is harmless.
11 We have already discussed the weaknesses in some parts of the reasoning. In general, the passage presents a fairly strong case for the legalization of cannabis, the weakest points being the failure to explore whether cannabis use might lead to use of hard drugs, and the questions over the connections between cannabis use and other crimes such as theft.

Summary: Assessing an argument

Analysing	Evaluating
1 Identify conclusion and reasons: **• look for 'conclusion indicators',** **• look for 'reason indicators',** **and/or** **• ask 'What is the passage trying to get me to accept or believe?'** **• ask 'What reasons, evidence is it using in order to get me to believe this?'**	**3 Evaluate truth of reasons/ assumptions.** **• how would you seek further information to help you do this?** **4 Assess the reliability of any authorities on whom the reasoning depends.** **5 Is there any additional evidence which strengthens or weakens the conclusion?**

2 Identify unstated assumptions:
- assumptions supporting basic reasons
- assumptions functioning as additional reasons,
- assumptions functioning as intermediate conclusions,
- assumptions concerning the meanings of words,
- assumptions about analogous or comparable situations,
- assumptions concerning the appropriateness of a given explanation.

- anything which may be true?
- anything you know to be true?

6 Assess the plausibility of any explanation you have identified.

7 Assess the appropriateness of any comparisons you have identified.

8 Can you draw any conclusions from the passage? If so, do they suggest that the reasoning in the passage is faulty?

9 Is any of the reasoning in the passage parallel with reasoning which you know to be faulty?

10 Do any of the reasons or assumptions embody a general principle? If so, evaluate it.

11 Is the conclusion well supported by the reasoning? If not, can you state the way in which the move from the reasons to the conclusion is flawed? Use your answers to questions 5 to 10 to help you do this.

Exercise 20: Ten longer passages to evaluate

Now you can try your hand on the following passages. Use the same eleven steps shown in the summary that we used in assessing the arguments about science versus theology and about the legalization of cannabis.

1 Cry-babies and colic

Some mothers suffer agony from incessantly crying babies during the first three months of life. Nothing the parents do seems to stem the flood. They usually conclude that there is something radically, physically wrong with the infants and try to treat them accordingly. They are right, of course, there is something physically wrong; but it is probably effect rather than cause.

The vital clue comes with the fact that this so-called 'colic' crying ceases, as if by magic, around the third or fourth month of life. It vanishes at just the point where the baby is beginning to be able to identify its mother as a known individual.

A comparison of the parental behaviour of mothers with cry-babies and those with quieter infants gives the answer. The former are tentative, nervous and anxious in their dealings with their offspring. The latter are deliberate, calm and serene. The point is that even at this tender age, the baby is acutely aware of differences in tactile 'security' and 'safety', on the one hand, and tactile 'insecurity' and 'alarm' on the other. An agitated mother cannot avoid signalling her agitation to her new-born infant. It signals back to her in the appropriate manner, demanding protection from the cause of the agitation. This only serves to increase the mother's distress, which in turn increases the baby's crying. Eventually the wretched infant cries itself sick and its physical pains are then added to the sum total of its already considerable misery.

All that is necessary to break the vicious circle is for the mother to accept the situation and become calm herself. Even if she cannot manage this (and it is almost impossible to fool a baby on this score) the problem corrects itself, as I said, in the third or fourth month of life, because at that stage the baby becomes imprinted on the mother and instinctively begins to respond to her as the 'protector'. She is no longer a disembodied series of agitating stimuli, but a familiar face. If she continues to give agitating stimuli, they are no longer so alarming because they are coming from a known source with a friendly identity. The baby's growing bond with its parent then calms the mother and automatically reduces her anxiety. The 'colic' disappears.

(Desmond Morris, The Naked Ape, *New York: Dell Publishing Co. Inc. 1967, pp. 98–9)*

2 School team sports turn children into idle adults

Tom Wilkie

Encouraging competitive sport in schools is wrong and risks turning children into adult couch potatoes, a former Newcastle United footballer told the British Association yesterday.

Schools should offer swimming, aerobics and dance as well as competitive team games, Professor Neil Armstrong of Exeter University, said.

The Government emphasis on team games was putting girls off sport, he continued: 'The national curriculum discriminates against girls and promotes inactive lifestyles.'

Today's young people are 'the most sedentary generation of children we've ever had,' he warned. In a study of 743 children aged 10 to 16, whose activity levels were monitored continuously for four days at a time,

Professor Armstrong found that nearly half the girls and 38 per cent of the boys 'did not even experience the equivalent of a 10-minute brisk walk.'

'All studies show that active children are likely to become active adults,' he said. Today's children were not less fit than previous generations but that was because 'they haven't been around long enough . . . The problems will be in adult life.'

John Major, the Prime Minister, told the Tory party conference last year the national curriculum would 'put competitive games back at the heart of school life. More time must be devoted to team games.'

Professor Armstrong stressed that, as a former professional footballer, he was not anti-team games, but warned that the Government has got the balance wrong. 'We want children to adopt an active lifestyle which will be sustained when they move into adulthood,' he said, and team games were not the way to achieve that.

In many schools the PE curriculum for girls was dominated by netball and hockey, yet these were not activities which could be sustained after the girls left school nor was it what they did out of school hours: if they were physically active at all they would find a partner for badminton, or go swimming or even enrol in an aerobics class.

Boys entering secondary school tend to have an aerobic fitness level about 18 per cent greater than girls (as measured by peak oxygen consumption during exercise). But the difference in their fitness increases with age, so that boys are on average about 37 per cent fitter by the end of compulsory secondary schooling than girls.

'We have to get across the message that exercise and physical activity can be fun,' Professor Armstrong said. Getting girls to take more exercise was vital because the most important role model for children was their mother, so if today's girls were directed into a sedentary lifestyle it would set the model for their own children.

For boys, competitive sport was not doing much more than favouring those who matured early and were stronger and taller, he said.

*(*Independent*, 15 September 1995)*

3 Moralists

Richard D. North

The International Fund for Animal Welfare's (IFAW) full-page advertisements in the broadsheet newspapers are stiff-arming Sir Ian MacLaurin, the chairman of Tesco, because that firm sells Canadian salmon. The argument goes that if he boycotts the salmon, the Canadian government will stop the seal-bashing on its ice-floes.

However, it so happens that the seals in question are thousands of miles from the salmon we are asked to resist eating. It is also probable that a salmon's death from 'drowning' in air is more horrible than a seal's having its brain stove in. Not one in a thousand of the T-shirt moralists who respond to IFAW's shock tactics will know or care about such fine-tuned matters.

And yet it is not on those grounds alone that I loathe this campaign. Nor is it merely that consumer boycotts are (forgive me) usually a rather blunt instrument. It may be right to call for a boycott of a nation's products in order to stop some horror in that country. Conceivably one should not buy Nike shoes because they are made by cheap labour in Asia (though I fear the cheap labourers might not agree).

Possibly it is right to try to halt the French nuclear testing by refusing to buy the country's claret (though the French claret industry has enough problems with competition from heroically moral countries such as Australia and Chile). It may even be right to try to change the regime in Nigeria by boycotting Shell (though one fancies a Shell withdrawal would lead to worse environmental damage in the Niger delta).

IFAW's campaign goes beyond these ploys by asserting that Tesco (as opposed to the Tesco consumer) ought to make a moral choice about where to buy salmon. Worse, it also stigmatises the hapless Sir Ian. This latter problem looks partly to be his own fault: the advertisements quote him as saying in 1984 that the company should stand up and be counted (on what was actually a different issue), and so IFAW now appears to be asking for a degree of consistency from him.

Both practically and ethically, I am afraid that firms should never claim to be capable of being a force for good. And they certainly should not offer to censor products on behalf of consumers. That way lies the closure of almost all business and also an unwarranted control of customer choice.

Firms cannot pay the kind of wages some moralists might argue for; they cannot be as green as Greenpeace would like; they cannot be as virtuous in picking their trading partners overseas as civil rights campaigners would like. Firms operate in a morally and ecologically dubious world. Not merely are they often ill-placed to make the required judgements: provided they do not hide what they do, and where, it is someone else's business altogether to decide whether they should be allowed to trade in a particular way.

Firms can only hope to be decent citizens, and in their case that comes down to obeying the law. Firms make profits, governments make rules: that is a respectable ordering of things. What stinks about this advertisement is not that it may be a wrong-headed call for a consumer boycott. The creepiness much more consists in making a pariah of an individual who, were he to obey every exhortation of every pressure group, would have empty shelves, from which it follows that we would probably have empty larders.

I hope that Sir Ian enjoys his knighthood, and will heed a warning that going for a halo as well would be dangerous. More widely, the boss class in firms ought to think carefully before allowing their public relations people to fashion caring, goody-goody images for their enterprises: virtue is not something to be traded in.

(Independent, *20 November 1995)*

4 Time to consent to change

Edwina Currie says homosexual law is unjust and counterproductive

If politicians have learnt anything recently it is not to moralise about other people's behaviour. No doubt many colleagues, along with the public, deplore the whole idea of homosexuality. That doesn't mean we should ban it. We cannot simply write our personal moral attitudes into a law which applies blindly to everybody. It doesn't work anyway, and that sets the worst example of all for our young people. They soon get the idea that they can ignore great chunks of other law, too.

The argument for changing the law to reduce the age of consent for gay men from the present age of 21 can be put in a more pragmatic way. In a free society, the onus is on those who discriminate to explain its practical benefits. For example, we all want to shield youngsters – boys and girls – from predatory adults. Yet if a boy wished, today, to make a complaint about an unwanted homosexual approach, he would think twice about telling the authorities – for it would be *he* who was questioned, and he might well face charges himself. So the current law acts not to protect, but to enforce silence. Who would seek help in these circumstances?

We faced a dilemma in Department of Health in the mid-1980s when we needed to warn young gay men of the mortal dangers of promiscuity. Talking to them about safe sex, we realized, meant asking health workers to seek out boys who were seriously breaking the law. We decided to go ahead anyway, for safety's sake: if our Aids death figures are now lower than everyone predicted, that wise decision takes the credit. How much easier, and more effective, if criminality was not at issue.

We should be clear that 'consent' means exactly that. If consent is withheld, then sex is illegal. In recent years, to my relief, it has been accepted that when a woman says no, she is entitled to be taken at her word. The same applies to young men too. Then there is the pressure that can come from an older person or one in a position of authority. That happens when young girls are involved as well; homosexuals have no monopoly on unpleasant behaviour. But it's against the law, and will rightly stay that way.

The House of Commons might prefer to reduce the age of consent to 18 rather than 16. This has a neat air of compromise and would reduce the discrimination against many gay men: a substantial net gain. But it would not be just, and it would not stick. The position is illogical. How could anyone accept that a young man of 17 is capable of giving informed consent if he falls for a girl – to the point where he can marry – but not if his inclinations are the other way? By the time I was 16, I knew that I liked boys, and nothing whatever has dissuaded me since. My gay friends say the same. All the medical evidence suggests that sexuality is settled quite young, certainly before 18.

Some people will never accept that for many people homosexuality is a way of life. Isn't it a disease which should be wiped out? Shouldn't we be taking every step to avoid further infection, particularly of the young? That is the assumption underlying all our institutions, including the criminal law, which forbids all homosexual acts under the age of 21, even though both parties – long since old enough to vote, or join the forces, or sleep with a girl – have given informed consent.

I was astonished to discover that the Commons had never seriously debated change since the Sexual Offences Act of 1967 made homosexuality legal in England and Wales. Scotland did not follow until 1980, and it was banned in Ulster until 1982.

Here is an outmoded law which touches, at the most conservative estimate, a million of our fellow citizens who are gay. Such men pay their taxes and hold down jobs; their ranks have included distinguished actors, composers, writers and artists, soldiers and politicians. They run banks and businesses at the highest level. Yet on this one topic, their personal judgement is regarded as dangerous: the State decides who they may and may not love. Surely this is, and always has been, absolute nonsense.

Most countries have equal ages of consent, often lower than ours. In Italy it is 14; in Holland, Greece, France, Poland and Sweden it is 15; in Norway, Belgium, Portugal and Switzerland, 16. The German government has announced that it will introduce equal age legislation, and the Irish government did so successfully last spring, at 17. In none of these sober, intelligent countries did the dire events transpire which have been predicted for Britain.

Parliament is at its best when it faces a clear issue of conscience. The welfare and human rights of a large group of our voters are at stake. I have always sought equality and respect in my own life. I will now vote for equality for others, and hope for a clear result to carry this country forward.

(The Times, *13 January 1994)*

5 Gasping for breath

Geoffrey Lean investigates the causes of the asthma epidemic

[Emissions from car exhausts have been blamed for the childhood asthma epidemic sweeping the country. One in seven children now suffers from the disease, with 100,000 people admitted to hospital each year.]

Asthma is a modern disease. Records at the Westminster Hospital show that it admitted its first asthmatic child in 1910, and that the disease was rare until after the First World War. But then it began its rapid rise.

It is also a disease of civilisation – or, rather, of what passes for it in an increasingly Westernised world. Asthma is ten times as common, for example, in Australia as in China. It seems to occur more frequently in the developed parts of Israel than in the poor areas, to be rare in rural Africa, but to increase as Africans migrate to cities.

So scientists are looking for causes hidden in more affluent lifestyles. It is not easy, because asthma is a complex disease. For a start it often runs in families, so there seems to be a genetic component predisposing people to developing it. Nevertheless, many people with no family history of asthma still get it. People with asthma also have more sensitive airways, and scientists believe that these remain inflamed even when the victim feels well. What originally causes the inflammation remains a mystery, but it seems that attacks are triggered when something irritates them, releasing a cascade of chemicals which brings on the crisis. The airways constrict and the attack is under way.

There are several suspect triggers in the modern lifestyle. Passive smoking is perhaps the best established. Mothers who smoke are much more likely to have asthmatic children. But Dr Martin Partridge, the chief medical adviser to the National Asthma Campaign, says: 'If you stopped all smoking, this would have a relatively small effect on the disease.' Something – or some things – even bigger is to blame.

Fur from pet animals and pollen may trigger attacks, but the prime suspects are now comfort and cars. Comfort comes into it because it suits house dust mites, which can also provoke asthma: fitted carpets and soft furnishings provide homes for mites, and central heating and double glazing supply a congenial atmosphere.

Increasingly, however, research is implicating two pollutants from car exhausts: ozone and nitrogen dioxide. Ozone, a blue-tinged form of oxygen, may be a life-saver up in the stratosphere where it forms the layer that screens out the harmful ultra-violet rays of the sun. But it is a dangerous pollutant nearer ground level; tiny concentrations of it crack stretched rubber and, not surprisingly, harm delicate human tissue. Nitrogen dioxide has a similar effect; a government report suggested earlier this year that it caused the 'greatest concern' of any air pollutant.

The two combine to cover much of the country with damaging levels of pollution. Nitrogen dioxide levels build up in towns because of the traffic. Emissions from car exhausts have increased by 73 per cent since 1981, and last year a government study reported that 19 million Britons were exposed to pollution that exceeded EC guidelines. Ozone, which is also increasing, takes longer to form and drifts on the winds out to the countryside in the process: Britain's highest levels are often recorded at East Sussex's idyllic Lullington Heath.

Studies in the United States have linked ozone with lung damage and asthma, while research in Canada, Switzerland and Sweden has implicated nitrogen dioxide. Recent work at the East Birmingham Hospital has shown that when levels of either pollutant rise, more people have to be admitted with asthma attacks. The study shows that 'acute respiratory admissions' increase at pollution levels 'well within the current EC daily guidelines' adding that 'significant' numbers of people have become sick 'at these presumed safe levels.'

This month, Professor Robert Davies of St Bartholomew's Hospital has published new research which shows that both ozone and nitrogen dioxide damage the lining of the respiratory system (allowing triggering substances to penetrate), impair the cilia (the tiny hairs that clear infection from cells) and help the chemical cascade that brings on asthma attacks.

He says that evidence has built up so strongly over the past few months that 'there is now no doubt that air pollution exacerbates asthma.'

Dr Malcolm Green, chairman of the British Lung Foundation, said yesterday that 4,000 top chest specialists meeting this month reached a 'consensus' that air pollution made asthmatics worse. It is not yet agreed that pollution can cause asthma in people who have not already had the disease, but, says Dr Green, this is 'almost a matter of semantics.'

He explains: 'If pollution is making people with bad asthma worse, and makes those with a little suffer more attacks, it is quite likely that those on the threshold of asthma may be tripped over it.'

The pollution hits children hardest because they are much more vulnerable. Children under three breathe in twice as much air as adults for each pound of their body weight. Kids exercise more, and so take in more air – and more pollution. Their airways are narrower, and so more vulnerable to constriction. And, as their lungs are still maturing, pollution can affect them permanently, leading to a lifetime of breathing difficulties.

At St Catherine's School in Bletchingley, Surrey, a quarter of the children have asthma. Most parents blame the nearby M25 motorway and say the situation has got dramatically worse in the past five years.

Can cars be made cleaner? From January all new cars will have to be fitted with catalytic converters, honeycombs which fit on car exhausts to trap pollution. Once it was thought that they might solve the problem, but they are both too late and too little.

They are too late because Britain held up agreement on introducing them in the EC for five years. They are too little because, although they reduce pollution massively in ideal laboratory conditions, the real world is much more complicated.

Nearly two thirds of all pollutants are emitted in the first few minutes of each journey, when the car is started from cold – and the catalysts do not work until after this, when they have been warmed up. They will only be introduced gradually as new cars come on the road, and the effect will soon be overtaken by the increase in traffic. The best that civil servants hope for is a brief breathing space – a cut of perhaps 5 per cent in emissions – before the pollutants rise again, but even this is optimistic. A government report earlier this year concluded that levels of nitrogen dioxide might well not decrease at all in some built-up areas.

Any serious attempt to tackle the pollution will have to be much bolder. It would help if the Government induced manufacturers to market the cars that they have already designed which do twice as many miles to the gallon as the ones they put in the showrooms.

But a real solution will have to go further, and consciously turn away from what Mrs Thatcher once lauded as 'the great car economy'. Thirty years ago Professor Colin Buchanan warned that the growth of car ownership threatened 'a national emergency'. Since his warning, the number of cars on Britain's roads has more than doubled, from 8 million to 18 million. Over the next 30 years, ministers predict, it will more than double again.

If they are to get to grips with the asthma epidemic, ministers will have to curb the car and promote public transport, use planning restrictions to curtail out-of-town developments that draw traffic, and start to redesign cities so that people have to travel less to shop, play or work.

Grouse as we may about traffic jams and pollution, we seem quite prepared to put up with them to enjoy the car's convenience. We seem ready to sacrifice our trees, killed by acid rain. We seem ready to destroy our countryside and our cities. We even seem prepared to accept more than 4,000 deaths and nearly 50,000 serious injuries in traffic accidents each year. Will we, if the link with asthma is proved, be prepared also to sacrifice our children's health?

(Independent on Sunday, *10 October 1993)*

6 Judges who believe in therapy instead of punishment are undermining the basis of law

Janet Daley

Patrick Weighell assaulted his infant son regularly. During the first six weeks of the baby's life, Weighell inflicted 23 fractures which were finally discovered by a doctor. Left to look after his son for six hours a day, Weighell often became very angry. If the baby was difficult to change or feed, Weighell would deliberately squeeze or shake him in a way likely to cause pain and injury.

As the trial judge, Robert Pryor QC, said to Weighell rather superfluously, 'I am sure you lost your temper occasionally.' While few would disagree with this statement of the obvious, most of us part company with Judge Pryor on the appropriate legal response to such behaviour.

What the judge recommended was a course of 'anger management' therapy to be attended by Weighell while on 18 months probation. He is to receive no punishment as such; no custodial sentence, not even community service. What he will get is treatment for what is seen as an unacceptable personality trait. One of the reasons given by Judge Pryor for this lenient sentence is that Weighell had shown remorse. This remorse was principally manifested in the form of a letter to the court in which Weighell expressed a hope that the family might be reunited.

Given that the assaults on his son were inflicted repeatedly over the entire span of the baby's life until the law intervened, you may question how much remorse Weighell felt before being apprehended. If he did feel spontaneous regret for his appalling actions on each and every occasion, you may wonder why he did not then recognize himself to be an unfit person to care for a baby and take steps to remove the child from his own dangerous impulses.

But let us err on the side of charity and assume that Weighell's protestations of remorse are quite genuine. Should being sorry excuse you from punishment? True, it may mean you are less likely to repeat this particular offence – remorse suggests that you are already on the road to reform – but to eliminate punishment altogether suggests that the law is paying less attention to the quality of the act than to the emotions of the offender.

This theory is given credence by Judge Pryor's apparent assumption that Weighell was not so much a criminal as a victim of his own lack of self-control. His crime had no ulterior motive; it was not done premeditatedly for illicit gain like a robbery. It simply *consisted* of losing his temper. Therefore, treating his flawed personality was more to the point than any of the things which punishment is traditionally supposed to be about: retribution, deterrence or character reform.

In fact, there are many people who see virtually all crime in these terms: burglary, mugging and car theft – being symptoms of emotional or social deprivation – are also signs that the perpetrators are incapable of self-control. Any anti-social behaviour is a species of acting out one's frustrations – a favourite notion of those therapists to whom Judge Pryor has entrusted Patrick Weighell. But I do not wish to pursue the wider debate about whether individuals, as opposed to the social conditions which formed them, are responsible for their acts.

The Weighell sentence raises a more specialised argument. If people committing unquestionably criminal acts – such as assaulting a baby – regularly become cases for treatment rather than punishment, then the basis of our system of criminal law is fundamentally changed.

As it stands, the purpose of the law is to prohibit certain acts, not to evaluate and reconstruct personalities. Of course, punishment may be reduced by mitigating factors. Stealing food when you are hungry is an obvious example.

But to refrain from punishment because the criminal is of a particular temperament, or has a certain susceptibility, is to remove the idea of guilt as the basis of criminal prosecution. Of course, the crime of baby-battering is likely to be committed by the short tempered. How many baby-batterers are not, by definition, out of control when they act? Should none of them be punished?

Is 'baby-battering' not a crime at all but the symptom of a parent who needs treatment? There are those who would say so, but their view is not usually associated with free societies. If crime is defined not as wrong-doing, but as personality disorder or social problem, then the object of the law is to diagnose rather than to punish. And this is, in fact, the practice of modern totalitarian societies who regard mind-control techniques, such as enforced 're-education' as the appropriate way to deal with any deviation from socially accepted behaviour.

Psychological treatment may look like a benign alternative to imprisonment, but in a democracy the law exists to enforce an agreed set of rules, not to reshape people's temperaments. The courts are supposed to assume that we all have free-will, and confine themselves to judging our actions. This assumption may sometimes be wrong, but it is less dangerous than presuming to rearrange our minds.

7 When the men came home

Gerald de Groot

In the sixties, British social historians were inclined to agree with Lenin that war is the great locomotive of history. The changes wrought by the Great War, it was argued, were tremendous. Nowadays, though, the idea seems more suited to its era – the decade of hope, progress and flared trousers. In the subdued Nineties, it is Britain's resistance to change that seems more striking.

Change did occur during the Great War. But countervailing forces were also at work. War was seen as an extraordinary event that brought a temporary tolerance for disruption and the armistice was accompanied by a widespread desire, among all classes, to return to normal. The extent to which normality was restored became the gauge of how worthwhile the sacrifices had been. After all, war is seldom fought to change society, but more often to preserve it.

The strength of resistance to change in Britain becomes clear from the subsequent fortunes of the two groups that supposedly benefited most from the Great War: the working class and women. According to conventional myth, both gained a sense of identity that was eventually converted into political power. Thus, in the trenches, millions of British workers mixed with middle-class officers who learnt to appreciate their worth. They were rewarded with a larger piece of the political pie.

But the belief in the great camaraderie of the trenches comes from reading too much Wilfred Owen. The Army took great pains to ensure that social barriers, deemed essential for discipline, did not fall. Trench officers had servants, better food and medical care, more frequent leave and their own brothels. If there was harmony in the trenches it was because subservient working-class soldiers did what they were told.

On the home front, workers derived some benefit from the scarcity of labour. Because skill differentials were relaxed, unskilled workers enjoyed the greatest improvement in their standard of living. This meant that the working class became more homogenous. But that is not the same as political solidarity. Nor did the rise of working-class consciousness automatically imply support for the Labour Party. The success of the Conservatives since 1918 might even suggest that increased consciousness could incline a worker towards the Tories.

Historians have too often imposed their own preconceptions on the workers they have studied. They have tended to assume, for instance, that the strikes on Clydeside and elsewhere were attempts to derive political advantage from the scarcity of labour, when they were in fact motivated by simple bread-and-butter issues. Inflation had outstripped wage increases. When the situation became intolerable, workers downed tools. When the Government made mild concessions, they went obediently back to work.

The most important consideration motivating the workers during the war was not socialist solidarity, but patriotism. There has been a massive – and futile – effort to prove that the 1914 rush to volunteer was inspired by gross militarism, widespread unemployment, or anything but patriotism. That the workers were patriotic is demonstrated by the virtual cessation of strikes from March to July 1918, when the German army was threatening to overrun the British. Clearly, the country's safety came before the workers' self-interest.

If the war radicalised the workers, why did the Conservatives dominate government for all but three of the inter-war years? Why did the workers tolerate a land unfit for heroes? Because the British working class was the most patriotic, subservient and apolitical in Europe, and this was unaltered by the Great War. Even if the working class emerged from the war a little more combative, workers derive power from scarcity of labour – and from 1918 to 1939 labour was anything but scarce.

The gains made by women during the Great War have also been exaggerated. According to myth, women left demeaning jobs in domestic service to take up employment in munitions factories. Their important work gave them independence, a sense of self-worth, improved status, and eventually political power – the right to vote.

The reality was quite different. A munitions factory was hardly the place to encourage self-belief. The work was unskilled, repetitive and dangerous. Women lost hair, their skin turned yellow and many were killed in factory explosions. They were paid better than they had been before the war, but they were not universally appreciated. Little effort was made to cater to their needs with separate washrooms or creches.

After the war, women workers were told to make way for returning soldiers. As one newspaper editorial remarked: 'The idea that, because the state called for women to help the nation, the state must continue to employ them is too absurd to entertain [. . .] women formerly in domestic service should have no difficulty finding vacancies'. Placements in domestic occupations increased by 40 per cent in 1919 over the year before. Nor did the war have any significant long-term effect upon the number of women in work. In 1921, 30.8 per cent of women were employed, down from 32.3 per cent 10 years earlier.

As the war demonstrated, a woman gains status when she performs a task previously reserved for men. But after the war that status disappeared if a woman surrendered her job to a returning soldier. Two areas of employment to which men did not return were those of shop assistants and office clerks. When these became predominantly female professions, they lost their status. War, because it is essentially masculine, can result in a step backward for women. Moreover, negative images of women abound in wartime: gossip-mongers whose loose lips sink ships, prostitutes who spread venereal disease, adulterers who cheat on soldier husbands.

Perhaps the most important effect of the Great War upon women was the massive increase in the marriage and birth rate after 1918. One would hesitate to conclude that women had an entirely free choice in the matter, but many may have welcomed the change from munitions worker to mother. Whether willingly or under duress, however, women returned to the status quo.

They did get the vote. But it is dangerous to assume that they would not have done so with equal despatch had there not been a war. Besides, the women who were enfranchised – property owners over 30 – were generally not the ones who filled the shells. And the clause giving votes to women was designed in part to limit the political effect of the 1918 voting act that removed most of the restrictions on male enfranchisement. Since the newly enfranchised men were mostly working class, and so expected to vote Labour, it was felt that granting the vote to middle-class women over 30 would be a counterweight.

One could cite many similar examples of war-induced social change being channelled, cushioned and blocked. Who is to blame? The idea of a great conservative conspiracy by a monolithic 'establishment' is too hard to swallow. Probably it has to be accepted that people generally harbour a preference for stability and tradition. Victory may in fact have encouraged a dangerous assumption that all was well at home and allowed antiquated social patterns to persist. If war is indeed the locomotive of history, the rolling stock in this case proved true to its British type – prone to delay and cancellations.

(Independent, *12 November 1993*)

8 Five reasons for a life of less crime

Hamish McRae

Crime. We all worry about it. President Bill Clinton used his State of the Union address this week to pledge an attack on it. Here in Britain both political parties realize that they must respond to public fears of it. The fear in America is that the very fabric of society is under siege. The fear here, where crime is lower, is that we might go down the American route.

Yet it is perfectly possible – indeed highly probable – that in Britain at least we are at one of those great turning points that occur every couple of generations: that crime, having risen inexorably since the Fifties, is now about to start a long period of decline, similar to the period from the 1830s onwards through most of the last century. Here are five reasons why this might be so.

The first is demography. Most crime is committed by young men. In 1986 there were more than 2.4 million men aged 20 to 24 in the UK, a figure which had risen from less than 2 million in 1976. This figure is now falling fast. By 1991 it was less than 2.3 million and it is projected to fall to just over 1.9 million by 1996 and slightly above 1.8 million by 2001. This is a big swing: 1.8 million will have to work roughly one-third harder to commit as many offences as 2.4 million did in the mid-Eighties.

That is a tall order. Even if these young men are even more criminally inclined than the mid-Eighties batch, and commit 10 or 15 per cent more offences per person, the crime rate will still come down.

Next, there is the trend in unemployment. Of course some of the most spectacular crimes, giant frauds for example, are committed by people in work. But there is undoubtedly some relationship between unemployment and crime, if only because people working 40 hours a week have 40 fewer hours to do anything else. The likely trend of unemployment deserves a column itself, but the demographic change ought to reduce unemployment among the young.

In any case, looked at from a long historical viewpoint the high unemployment rates of the Eighties throughout Europe are unusual. The very low rates of the Fifties are also unusual, but a return to the 5 to 8 per cent range by the end of this decade is quite possible.

Third: technology. We are only just beginning to realize the full implications of devices such as the video camera, which could be as important in cutting crime as the invention of street lighting in the last century. The pioneering work here has been done in the Scottish town of Airdrie, which introduced cameras in November 1992. A dramatic drop in crime resulted. Since then a number of cities and towns have introduced surveillance schemes or are about to. A set of cameras in Bournemouth cut vandalism to such an extent that the system paid for itself in little more than a year. The biggest such experiment is in Glasgow, and if that achieves similar results, it will show that video cameras are as effective in giant cities as in small and medium-sized ones.

Naturally there are many other technologies that will help further: technologies as varied as a national DNA register, car immobilisers and the etching of photos on credit cards. But video cameras are the big success story of the past couple of years.

Fourth: policing. It is monstrously unfair to say so, but during the Eighties the police seemed almost to boast about rising crime. They behaved like a data collection agency; the more crime they could record, the more they needed more people, higher pay and faster cars to fight it. Instead of being ashamed of their failure, they blustered on about failures of society.

It is hard to generalise, but attitudes really seem to have changed. In some specific areas, like football matches, policing has visibly improved. My colleagues on the sports desk point out that the hooting and singing by some fans during the one-minute silence for Sir Matt Busby seemed shocking because it contrasted with generally better behaviour at football matches in recent years. This they attributed not to any change in the fans but in the policing of them. Pressure on the police is probably improving performance in other areas too.

Finally: change in social attitudes, in culture, in what we all expect of people. It is hard to pin this down, but something is clearly happening. People are not only more worried; they are more angry and they are becoming more organized. In Scotland, where crime fell quite sharply last year and clear-up rates have risen, the shift is attributed by police to a number of factors, including neighbourhood watch schemes and generally better co-operation with the public.

Individually, these five points might not be sufficient to turn round what has been a steady and alarming rise in crime. There are offsetting negative forces that I have not discussed, including the greater availability of firearms which are now flooding out of the old Soviet empire; greater freedom of movement within Europe and between Britain and the rest of the world; probably still rising levels of drug abuse; the danger that better job prospects for young qualified people will leave the unqualified even more excluded and alienated.

But taken together, the five factors cutting crime ought to have greater impact than each would have individually. Once it is clear that crime really is coming down, the word gets around and a virtuous circle is established. Police and public become more confident: detection rates rise; it becomes harder to dispose of stolen goods, so the returns fall. The risk–reward ratio is thus tilted against the aspiring criminal, and crime simply becomes an unattractive proposition.

All this, please note, has nothing to do with politicians and nothing to do with the law.

The reaction of most people to this argument would probably be that, if it proves true, it should be warmly welcomed: crime is bad. It may sound odd, then, to end with a warning.

There will be costs to falling crime. The sort of changes outlined above will involve some restriction of individual liberties. It is not just that we will have to become used to being watched as we shop, or simply walk up the street. We may, a generation from now, find ourselves in a more censorious society: one which imposes greater social control on our behaviour and which becomes much more hostile to people who do not conform to what other people regard as normal and proper. Our society may become safer, but it may also become less exuberant, less interesting, and in some senses, less free.

(Independent, *27 January 1994)*

9 Warning: some statistics can drive you mad

Peter Popham

After an absence of nearly a year, the mad cow is back in the headlines. 'Experts fear 1.5 million "mad cows" eaten', brays the *Sunday Times*. 'New fear of mad cow link' declared Monday's *Daily Mail*.

The good news is that these sensational stories are erected on statistical matchwood. BSE, popularly known as 'mad cow disease', continues to afflict herds of British cows – 9,602 diseased cows have so far been slaughtered this year – despite the drastic efforts of the Ministry of Agriculture, Food and Fisheries to uproot it. But that is a problem for the farmer and the taxpayer who compensates him, and a declining one at that: BSE numbers have been falling since 1992, when 36,681 British cows were affected. It is not directly a problem for the consumer.

The consumer's anxiety is focused not on these figures but on the human equivalent of BSE, the terrible degenerative brain ailment which culminates in death, Creutzfeldt–Jakob Disease (CJD). If these figures were to show a steep rise, there would be good reason for public alarm. But last year in Britain only 54 people died from the disease, a figure comparable to Germany (58) and France (47) where BSE is practically unknown. Deaths in Britain have increased substantially in the past few years, but it is plausibly argued that this is because the National CJD Surveillance Unit in Edinburgh, galvanised by public concern, has intensified its efforts and thereby detected more cases.

The real reason for the mad cow's return to the headlines is that scourge of the age, the misdirected fax. Doctors and scientists on the government Spongiform Encephalopathy Advisory Committee mis-faxed a secret report, which was obtained by the *Daily Mail*, on recent cases of CJD, noting that a fourth farmer had apparently contracted the disease and 'the Committee concluded that it was difficult to explain this as simply a chance phenomenon. There is a statistical excess of cases in cattle farmers compared to the general population . . .'. Yet even this could reasonably be dismissed as scholarly excess of scruple: the incidence of CJD among farmers, after all, is no more than two per million. And, statistically, the group most at risk from the disease is not farmers but vicars, with 11.8 cases per million. This says more about statistics than it does about the Church of England.

But the success of the government last year in reversing the German ban on imports of British beef, and the persistently low incidence of CJD, should not deflect attention from the fact that certain urgent questions remain unanswered.

Most importantly, if, as has been proved, BSE can spread to cats, ostriches, antelopes, pumas and cheetahs – in all cases, it appears, through the use of infected feed in zoos – how can anybody declare with certainty that it will not cross, or has not already crossed, the species line to humans too?

Headlines such as the *Sunday Times*'s may invite mockery, but the incubation period for kuru, a similar brain disease to CJD found among a particular cannibalistic tribe in Papua New Guinea, [is] about 30 years. We cannot with absolute certainty rule out the possibility of a very nasty epidemic of CJD in Britain sometime around 2015.

Secondly, why has the disease continued to ravage the British herds five, six and seven years after the ban on infected feeds and the wholesale slaughter of infected animals?

Thirdly, why should prudent people continue to give credence to the reassurances of the MAFF – a ministry which has presided over a succession of agribusiness disasters, all brought about by its own policies? When a government department is, like MAFF, under intense pressure to shore up an important industry, would not the consumer be safer off just saying no to beef?

As part of the fever for deregulation that gripped Whitehall in the early Eighties, producers of cattlecake – which routinely included minced-up bits of sheep and cattle carcasses as well as grain – were enabled to cut out a couple of key steps in the manufacturing process. As a result, tissue of brains of sheep which were infected with the long-established sheep disease scrapie managed to survive into the finished feed, and thereby made their way into the stomachs of cows.

[BSE in cows] was first identified in 1986 and decimated herds all over the country before, in the summer of 1988, the Secretary of State for Agriculture, John MacGregor, decided on drastic action and instructed all affected animals to be slaughtered. But it didn't work. The disease continued unabated.

The spate of sensationalising stories of the past few days has done the useful service of reminding us that the mad cow problem had stubbornly refused to go away. Most alarming of all was the fact that, as the continuing deaths served to rub in, the cause of the epidemic had not necessarily been isolated. The ministry insisted that infected feed must be at the root of the problem. But when an organic farmer from Somerset called Mark Purdey asserted that BSE was caused by something quite different – by the use of organo-phosphorous treatments for other animal ailments – the ministry's leading scientists paid him the compliment of listening to his case. They reject his thesis. But nobody has yet succeeded in isolating the positive agent of the virus. A great deal of mystery and ignorance continues to surround it.

Whether infected sheep or organo-phosphorous treatments are to blame, it is beyond doubt that the cause of the problem, seen in the larger context, is the industrialisation of farming.

Without much fanfare, a number of People Who Know in the medical profession have given up eating beef; the latest was Sir Bernard Tomlinson, architect of the NHS reforms, who recently admitted he was less sure than previously that BSE could not jump the species barrier. Those who value their lives would do well to study their example.

*(*Independent*, 25 October 1995)*

10 A social divide based on merit

Peter Saunders

Is there a relationship between intelligence and social class? This is the delicate question addressed by the American right-wing policy analyst, Charles Murray, in his new book, *The Bell Curve*. Predictably, reaction has been fierce and mostly hostile.

For the past 10 years, Mr Murray has been warning of the emergence of an ill-educated, dependent and disaffected 'underclass' in America and Britain. Now he has gone one step further, suggesting IQ tests show that the American underclass is on average less intelligent than other people, and that this difference is reproduced from generation to generation.

In one sense there is nothing new about Mr Murray's findings, for we have known for a long time that IQ scores vary on average between social classes. When Britain still had the 11-plus examination, children of professional and managerial parents recorded average IQ scores of 113, compared with an average of around 96 for the children of unskilled manual workers. Similar differences have been recorded in the US and elsewhere.

Many people, however, do not accept IQ scores as a valid measure of intelligence. They claim that lower-class children are not less intelligent; they simply perform worse in tests which are biased towards those from middle-class backgrounds.

Since the argument has never been resolved between people who accept IQ tests as valid and people who do not, there seems little point in Mr Murray using such tests to investigate differences in intelligence; the validity of the results will always be disputed.

There is, however, another way of analysing the link between social class and intelligence which does not rely on measuring IQs. Instead, we begin by comparing the proportion of working-class children who make it into the middle class with the proportion of middle-class children who manage to stay there.

A survey of 10,000 men carried out by researchers at Nuffield College, Oxford in the 1970s found substantial movement between the classes in Britain, but also revealed a clear link between social background and occupational success. Nearly six out of every 10 boys born to middle-class fathers made it into the middle class themselves, but this was true for fewer than two in 10 boys from the working class. Middle-class children are thus three to four times more likely to succeed.

The Nuffield team believed that such a large disparity must be due to the influence of social background. This was, however, never demonstrated, for the study did not attempt to investigate the intelligence of the people it surveyed. We must therefore consider whether a difference in success as great as 4:1 in favour of middle-class children could be explained by middle-class parents producing more intelligent offspring.

Unless we are willing to assume that we are all born with exactly the same intellectual capacity (in which case any of us could have written the plays of Shakespeare or discovered the theory of relativity), we have to accept that innate differences of intelligence exist, and that such differences will tend to be passed on from parents to their children. Of course, just as tall parents can sometimes produce short children, bright parents can sometimes produce dull ones. The point, however, is that on average, intelligent parents are more likely to produce bright offspring.

This has a crucial implication. Imagine a society where competition for jobs was genuinely open, and where the brightest children were recruited to the top jobs irrespective of their social origins. In such a society, not only would the middle class be more intelligent than the working class, but it would tend to produce more than its fair share of bright children who would themselves be eligible for middle-class positions. In a truly meritocratic society, we would thus *expect* to find some association between class origins and occupational success.

How strong would this link be? Could it produce differences in the order of three or four to one?

Fifty years ago, the professional middle class in Britain was quite small – about one in seven of the workforce. Had entry to the middle class depended solely on intelligence, it would have required an IQ of around 116, for about one-seventh of the population has an IQ this high.

One generation later, the middle class has expanded to around one-quarter of the employed population. This next generation would therefore have required an IQ of 109 or thereabouts to secure a middle-class position based on intelligence.

What is the likelihood of parents with an IQ of at least 116 producing children with an IQ as high as 109? The answer is that about six out of every 10 of their children would score this high. So if class recruitment in these two generations had been based entirely on intelligence, about six out of every 10 middle-class children would have been bright enough to qualify for middle-class entry.

How many working-class children would qualify? Based on the same calculations, working-class parents would have an IQ no higher than 102, and fewer than two out of 10 of their children could be expected to have an IQ as high as the 109 required for middle-class entry.

Remarkably, these figures correspond almost exactly to the findings of the Nuffield team. The survey found that middle-class children were three or four times more likely to succeed than working-class children, but this is exactly what would happen if intelligence alone determined class membership.

Two important conclusions follow from this. First, Britain looks surprisingly like a society divided into classes on the basis of talent. The pattern of social mobility is broadly consistent with what should happen in a perfectly open society with recruitment based solely on intelligence.

The second conclusion is that we do not need to do IQ tests to find evidence supporting the link between social class and intelligence. The close approximation between what would happen under open competition and what does happen in Britain indicates that ability probably does coincide to a large extent with class positions. This lends strong support to Mr Murray's claim of a link between low average intelligence and low class position.

What it does *not* do is support Mr Murray's additional claim that intelligence is also linked to race. Social classes are recruited through competition and therefore change their membership over time, but racial groups are fixed at birth. The class system can sift each generation by intelligence, but there is no comparable process through which a link between race and intelligence could be sustained.

(Independent, *25 October 1994)*

Answers to Exercise 20 are given on p. 159.

Exercise 21: Topics for constructing your own arguments

Now that you have worked through the analysis and evaluation of other people's reasoning, you should be confident that you can construct good arguments of your own. Here are some suggestions of topics on which you can put your well-developed skills into practice.

1 Write an argument either in favour of or against single-sex schools.
2 Write an argument in favour of improving and extending rail services in Britain.
3 Write an argument either in favour of or against legalizing soft drugs.
4 Write a passage about the benefits and disadvantages of our widespread use of the motor car. Come to a conclusion as to whether the motor car is a good thing or a bad thing.
5 Write an argument about the role, if any, that families could play in reducing crime.
6 Write an argument either in favour of or against restrictions of the freedom of the press to write about the lives of individuals.
7 Write an argument about whether the monarchy in Britain is a good thing.
8 Write an argument about whether capital punishment should be reintroduced in Britain.

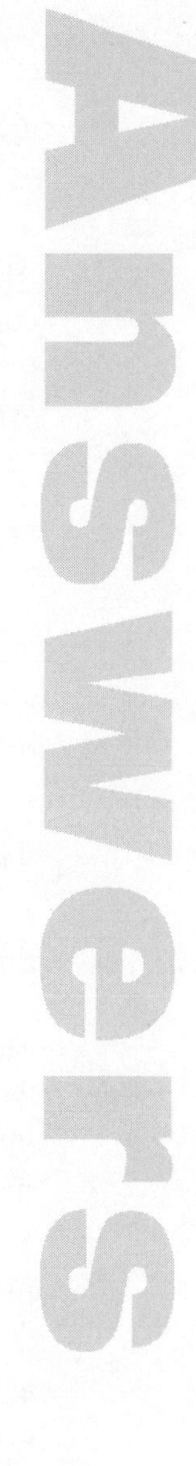

Answers to exercises

Exercise 1: Identifying arguments and conclusions

1 This is an argument, and the conclusion is the final sentence of the passage. The passage contains the 'conclusion indicator' word 'should' in two places – in the second sentence and in the final sentence. However, the second sentence is not a conclusion, because no evidence or reasons are given for believing that parents should be capable of teaching the skills – it is simply taken for granted that they should. The final sentence is making a recommendation to spend money on training parents rather than spending it on nursery education, *based on the reasons that* children will need these skills before starting school, and parents should be capable of teaching them. To rewrite the passage, simply insert 'So' or 'Therefore' before the last sentence.

2 This is not an argument. It makes three unconnected statements about children aged under five – that they learn more at this time than at any other time in their lives, that many receive pre-school education, and that some attend school. None of these statements gives any reason to believe either of the others.

3 This is not an argument. It simply gives information about differences between the diets of red squirrels and the diets of

grey squirrels. Note that the word 'cannot' appears in the passage, but it is not being used to indicate a conclusion – it simply reports a fact.

4 This is an argument, and the conclusion is the second sentence. The word 'should' in this sentence indicates that a recommendation is being made to compensate farmers for taking riverside farmland out of production. The rest of the passage provides the reasons for this – that it would save money and benefit the environment. The passage can be rewritten as follows:

> Millions of pounds of public money are spent defending riverside farmland from flooding. Some of this money could be given to farmers to compensate them for taking such land out of production. This would save money and would benefit the environment, since if rivers were allowed to flood, their natural flood plains would provide wetland meadows and woodland rich in wildlife. So some of the money spent on defending riverside farmland from flooding should be given to farmers to compensate them for taking such land out of production.

5 This is not an argument. It simply reports some items of information about the weather.

6 This is an argument, and the conclusion is the final sentence. Notice that this sentence begins with the phrase 'This indicates', suggesting that a conclusion is being drawn from the evidence about increases in sightings of bald eagles. The conclusion also relies on the assumption (not explicitly stated) that if there has been an increase in sightings, there must be more eagles. To rewrite the passage, simply insert 'So' before the last sentence.

7 This is not an argument. It simply gives three different items of information about people who have computer skills – that the demand for them is growing, that their numbers are increasing, and that sometimes they need further training. None of these statements gives any reason to believe the others.

8 This is an argument. It may be more difficult to see this than with other examples, because the conclusion is not set out in a simple sentence. Yet there clearly is some reasoning going on, and a recommendation is being made that we should not lower speed limits in order to deal with the problem of unsafe drivers. The reason given for this is that to do so would inconvenience the majority who drive safely. The passage could be rewritten as follows:

> Although we could reduce road accidents by lowering speed limits, and making greater efforts to ensure that such limits are enforced, this would inconvenience the majority who drive safely. Therefore, it would be an unacceptable solution to the problem of careless drivers who are unsafe at current speed limits.

9 This is an argument, and the conclusion is the first sentence. The word

'should' in this sentence tells us that a recommendation is being made. The rest of the passage gives the reasons for this recommendation. The word 'therefore' appears in the last sentence, but it is not introducing a main conclusion here. You can see that the passage makes sense as an argument if rewritten in the following way:

> A dollar to a poor man means more than a dollar to a rich man – in that it meets more urgent needs and, therefore, produces more happiness. So the same amount of wealth will yield more happiness if it is distributed widely than if it is divided with great inequality. The purpose of distributing wealth must be to produce more happiness. Therefore wealth should be distributed more evenly.

10 This is an argument, and the conclusion is the second sentence. It may seem odd that the conclusion is simply the sentence 'But this is not so.' However, it is clear that most of the passage gives information which tells us why we should accept that the risk of getting lung cancer is *not* the greatest risk to health from smoking. Here is a rewritten version which sets out the conclusion more clearly:

> Government campaigns against smoking are always based on the assumption that the greatest risk to health from smoking is the risk of getting lung cancer. It is true that heavy smoking roughly doubles a person's chance of dying of heart disease, whereas it increases the chance of dying from lung cancer by about ten times. But we have to take into account the fact that there is a much higher incidence of heart disease than of lung cancer in the general population. This means that for every smoker who develops lung cancer, there will be about three who die of self-induced heart disease. So it is not true that the greatest risk to health from smoking is the risk of getting lung cancer.

Exercise 3: Identifying reasons

1 The answer is (c).

(c) supports the recommendation to pay blood donors by mentioning an advantage of doing so – that it would remedy or reduce the shortage of blood donors by encouraging more people to become donors.

(a) does not support the conclusion, because it suggests that the Blood Donor service may not be able to afford to pay donors.

(b) may look tempting, but it does not support the conclusion, unless we assume that people should always be paid for helping others. It suggests that for many people, there is no need to pay them in order to motivate them to give blood.

2 The answer is (b).

(b) supports the conclusion since if employers ignore the importance of applicants' personalities, they may appoint someone with an unsuitable personality which cannot be changed. If, however, they appoint someone with a suitable personality, they can easily teach this person the necessary skills.

(a) does not support the conclusion, because if both personalities and vital skills are subject to change, then neither provides a good basis for choosing someone for a job.

(c) counts against the conclusion, because it suggests that personality differences between candidates are not very important (since everyone can develop a good personality), and also that for some jobs, those which involve skills which not everyone can acquire, differences between candidates in terms of their skills are very important.

3 The answer is (a).

(a) supports the conclusion by mentioning a disastrous possible consequence for light-skinned people of exposure to the sun – the likelihood of getting skin cancer.

(b) is not relevant to the conclusion, since it mentions the effect of exposure to the sun only for dark-skinned people, and the conclusion concerns only the effect for light-skinned people.

(c) does not support the conclusion. It mentions a way in which light-skinned people can avoid some exposure to the sun – by using sun creams. But it does not say anything about why they should avoid exposure.

4 The answer is (a).

(a) supports the conclusion by pointing out an economic benefit of installing insulation – reducing fuel costs. So even if it is expensive to install insulation, in the long run you may save money by doing so.

(b) does not support the conclusion, since it does not mention an economic benefit of installing insulation. It simply refers to the benefit in terms of comfort.

(c) does not support the conclusion, because it mentions a disadvantage of some types of insulation – that they can cause damp. This gives no reason to think that installing insulation is economical. In fact it suggests that it may lead to extra costs, for treatment of damp.

5 The answer is (c).

(c) supports the conclusion by showing that imprisonment of young offenders leads to an increase in crime, since it makes them more likely to re-offend.

(a) does not support the conclusion that young offenders should not be imprisoned. It simply suggests a way of using their time in prison constructively – to teach them job skills.

(b) does not support the conclusion, because it focuses only on overcrowding in prisons and the expense of building new ones, whereas the conclusion focuses on the reduction of crime as a reason for not using imprisonment for young offenders.

6 The answer is (c).

(c) supports the conclusion by showing that it was physically impossible for Sam to have committed the murder.

(a) does not support the conclusion, because even if Sally both wanted to commit the murder and could have done it, this does not show that Sam could not have done it.

(b) does not support the conclusion, since Sam could have committed the murder even if he had nothing to gain by doing so.

7 The answer is (b).

(b) supports the conclusion by showing that those who have a vegetarian diet avoid eating something which can be bad for health – the animal fats which can cause heart disease.

(a) does not support the conclusion, because it mentions only a deficiency of vegetarian diet – the lack of certain vitamins – which might suggest that a vegetarian diet could be bad for health.

(c) does not support the conclusion because it mentions something which is beneficial to health, but which is absent from vegetarian diets.

8 The answer is (b).

(b) supports the conclusion by showing that something undesirable would happen if many parents did not have their children vaccinated against polio – that there would be outbreaks of the disease every few years.

(a) does not support the conclusion, because it simply tells us what some parents think about the risk of side effects from the vaccine. This gives us no information about the benefits of vaccination.

(c) on its own does not support the conclusion. It might suggest that there is little need to have children vaccinated against polio, since the risk of becoming infected is very low. However, the reason why the risk is low may be because there has been a high level of vaccination amongst the population. If this information were added to (c), (c) could function as part of the reasoning to support the conclusion.

9 The answer is (a).

(a) supports the conclusion because if non-swimmers avoid activities in which there is a high risk of drowning, and swimmers engage in these activities, then this could explain why amongst those who drown there are more swimmers than non-swimmers.

(b) does not support the conclusion, because it does not say whether most of those who fail to wear life-jackets are swimmers.
(c) does not support the conclusion, because it says nothing about non-swimmers. It explains why even those who can swim may drown, but this gives us no reason to think that amongst those who drown there will be more swimmers than non-swimmers.

10 The answer is (c).
(c) supports the conclusion by showing that some chewing gums cause tooth decay.
(a) does not support the conclusion, because it simply tells us about the chewing gums which can be good for the teeth.
(b) does not support the conclusion, because it suggests chewing any type of gum can have some good effect on the teeth.

Exercise 4: Identifying parts of an argument

In these answers, the reasons are numbered, 'reason 1, reason 2' and so on. It does not matter which number you give to which reason, so don't worry if you have numbered them differently. What matters is the relationship between reasons and intermediate conclusions, and between reasons and main conclusions.

1 The main conclusion in this argument is the last sentence, clearly signalled by the word 'So.' The rest of the argument is a little vague, but we could regard the first and second sentences as two reasons offered jointly in support of the conclusion, which would give the following structure:

Reason 1: The odds that a dangerous leak from a nuclear power plant could occur are so small as to be almost impossible to calculate.
Reason 2: I have as much chance of being seriously injured backing out of my drive as I would living next to a nuclear power plant for a year.

These two reasons taken together are intended to support:

Conclusion: So someone living next door to a nuclear power plant should feel 100 per cent safe.

However, this structure is debatable. Reason 1 may not be saying any more than Reason 2 says.

2 The main conclusion is the last sentence, signalled by the phrase 'That is why.' Notice the word 'because' in the second sentence, indicating a reason. The argument has the following structure:

Reason 1: Passive smoking causes cancer.

This is offered in support of:

> *Intermediate conclusion:* Smokers are putting our health at risk.

This intermediate conclusion, taken together with:

> *Reason 2:* The one third of people who smoke in public places are subjecting the rest of us to discomfort.

is offered in support of:

> *Main conclusion:* That is why it is time to ban smoking in public places.

The intermediate conclusion and reason 2 *could* be regarded as supporting the main conclusion independently, but the argument is stronger if they are taken as joint reasons for the conclusion.

3 The main conclusion is the last sentence, introduced by the conclusion indicator 'Hence.' We also find 'so' in the second sentence, indicating an intermediate conclusion. The argument has the following structure:

> *Reason 1:* From every effect the existence of the cause can be clearly demonstrated,

This is intended to support:

> *Intermediate conclusion:* So we can demonstrate the existence of God from His effects.

This, taken together with:

> *Reason 2:* The existence of God is not self-evident to us.

is intended to support:

> *Main conclusion:* Hence the existence of God, insofar as it is not self-evident to us, can be demonstrated from those of His effects which are known to us.

4 The passage is trying to convince us that matter has not always existed. This is evident from the phrase 'is scientific proof that.' The word 'So' which introduces the second sentence indicates that an intermediate conclusion is being drawn. The structure of the argument is as follows:

> *Reason 1:* Radioactive elements disintegrate and eventually turn into lead.

This is intended to support:

> *Intermediate conclusion:* So if matter has always existed there should be no radioactive elements left.

This is intended to support:

Main conclusion: The presence of uranium and other radioactive elements is scientific proof that matter has not always existed.

You could if you wished split up the final sentence as follows:

Reason 2: Uranium and other radioactive elements are present.

Then take this together with the intermediate conclusion to support:

Main conclusion: This is scientific proof that matter has not always existed.

5 In this example there are no conclusion indicators, so you have to consider what is the main point of which it is trying to convince you. This appears in the last sentence, and the rest of the passage is offered in support of this point, as follows:

Reason 1: A foetus's heart is beating by 25 days after fertilization.

Reason 2: Abortions are typically done 7 to 10 weeks after fertilization.

These two reasons are taken together to support:

Intermediate conclusion: Even if there were any doubt about the fact that the life of each individual begins at fertilization, abortion clearly destroys a living human being with a beating heart and a functioning brain.

This intermediate conclusion is intended to support:

Main conclusion: If the first right of a human being is the right to his or her life, the direct killing of an unborn child is a manifest violation of that right.

Note that the conclusion is hypothetical. You may have been tempted to think that the conclusion was simply that abortion is a violation of the right to life. But the passage does not definitely state that human beings have a right to life. It says that *if* they do, abortion (since it kills the foetus) violates that right.

6 The main conclusion, clearly signalled by 'Therefore', is the final sentence. The argument can be regarded as having the following structure:

Reason 1: It has always been the case in the past that new discoveries of mineral reserves have kept pace with demand.

Reason 2: At no time have the known reserves of minerals been as great as the total mineral resources of the world.

These two reasons, taken together, are intended to support:

Main conclusion: Therefore, even though at any given time we know of only a limited supply of any mineral, there is no reason for us to be concerned about running out of mineral resources.

Note that the example presented in the second sentence is being used to give some support to reason 1. But we have not shown this as a reason from which reason 1 follows, because one example could not be sufficient to establish a general claim such as reason 1, nor is it likely that the author of the argument thinks that the example does establish the general claim. It is being used in an illustrative way. You could include the second sentence in the argument structure by simply treating it as a part of reason 1.

7 The main conclusion is the first sentence, in which the word 'should' tells us that a recommendation is being made. The second and third sentences are straightforward reasons, but the fourth sentence is more complex. It contains a reason and an intermediate conclusion, and the reason is introduced by the word 'because.' We have to repeat some of the wording in order to make the structure complete, as follows:

> *Reason 1:* If sentences are as heavy for those who plead guilty to the charge of rape as for those who plead not guilty, there is nothing to lose by pleading guilty.

This is intended to support:

> *Intermediate conclusion:* If sentences are as heavy for those who plead guilty as for those who plead not guilty, all defendants will plead not guilty.

This intermediate conclusion is taken together with the following two reasons:

> *Reason 2:* For a victim of rape, appearing in court is a very distressing experience.
>
> *Reason 3:* If the defendant pleads guilty, the victim does not have to appear in court.

to give support to:

> *Main conclusion:* In rape cases, sentences should be lighter for those who plead guilty than for those who plead not guilty.

8 The main conclusion is the final sentence, and is clearly indicated by the word 'Thus.' The argument has the following structure:

> *Reason 1:* If imprisonment worked as a deterrent to potential criminals, the more people we had in prison to serve as examples, the more would their lesson be conveyed to those outside prison.
>
> *Reason 2:* But today we have record numbers of people in prison, and a crime rate which is growing, not decreasing.

These two reasons, taken together, are intended to support:

> *Main conclusion:* Thus, imprisonment is not an effective deterrent.

9 The main conclusion is the first sentence. You have to work this out by asking what is the main message which the passage is trying to convey. The only conclusion indicator in the passage – the word 'thus' in the fourth sentence – signals an intermediate conclusion. The structure of the argument is as follows:

> *Reason 1:* Experience shows that kidnap victims are less likely to be killed by their captors if the kidnapping is not reported.

This is intended to support:

> *Intermediate conclusion:* To report a kidnap can thus endanger a victim's life.

This intermediate conclusion is taken together with:

> *Reason 2:* If we do not pass legislation against publishing in these circumstances, some newspapers will continue to be irresponsible and will publish details of the kidnapping before the victim is released or rescued.

in order to support:

> *Main conclusion:* Those who oppose any and all restrictions on freedom of the press are wrong.

10 The main conclusion appears in the final sentence, introduced by the words 'I conclude that.' Here is one way in which the structure of this argument can be set out.

> *Reason 1:* [If killing an animal infringes its rights, then] never may we destroy, for our convenience, some of a litter of puppies, or open a score of oysters when nineteen would have sufficed, or light a candle in a summer evening for mere pleasure, lest some hapless moth should rush to an untimely end.
>
> *Reason 2:* Nay, we must not even take a walk, with the certainty of crushing many an insect in our path, unless for really important business!
>
> *Reason 3:* Surely all this is childish.

These three reasons can be regarded as being intended to support:

> *Intermediate conclusion:* It is absolutely hopeless to draw a line anywhere.

This intermediate conclusion is intended to support:

> *Main conclusion:* I conclude that man has an absolute right to inflict death on animals, without assigning any reason, provided that it be a painless death, but that any infliction of pain needs its special justification.

Exercise 7: Identifying assumptions in arguments

1 This passage concludes that there must be some innate differences between males and females in 'target-directed motor skills', on the grounds that even at the age of three, boys perform better than girls at these skills. The passage is clearly rejecting the other possible explanation which it mentions – that 'upbringing gives boys more opportunities to practise these skills.' The conclusion thus relies on the assumption that by the age of three boys cannot have had sufficient practice at these skills to account for their better performance.

The assumption can be stated as follows:

> Before the age of three, boys cannot have had sufficient practice at target-directed motor skills to account for the fact that they perform better at these skills than girls of the same age.

The assumption functions as an additional reason.

2 This passage concludes that allowing parents to choose the sex of their children could have serious social costs. The two reasons given for this are that it would result in more males who could not find female partners, and it would lead to an increase in violent crime (since most violent crimes are committed by males). However, these two results would occur only if there was an increase in the male to female ratio in the population. So these two reasons rely on the assumption that if parents were allowed to choose the sex of their children, there would be a greater tendency to choose male offspring than to choose female offspring.

The assumption can be stated as follows:

> If parents were able to choose the sex of their children, there would be more parents who chose to have boys than parents who chose to have girls.

This is an assumption which underlies the two basic reasons in the argument.

3 This argument concludes that the continued fall in house prices may have a beneficial effect. The reason given for this is that the middle classes will become enthusiastic campaigners for improvements in their environment. This reason is itself an intermediate conclusion, supported by the claim that when people live in a house for a long period of time, they develop a strong commitment to the local neighbourhood. This reason would not fully support the intermediate conclusion, without the assumption that if house prices continue to fall, the middle classes are likely to move house less frequently.

The assumption can be stated as follows:

> The continued fall in house prices is likely to lead to the typical middle-class home owner occupying a house for a long period of time.

The assumption functions as an additional reason.

4 There are a number of unstated moves in this argument. The following outline of the structure of the argument identifies them.

Assumption 1: The alarm did not wake me.

Reason 1: The alarm easily wakes me if it goes off.

These two are taken together to support an unstated:

Intermediate conclusion 1 (Assumption 2): The alarm did not go off.

This in turn supports:

Intermediate conclusion 2: If the money has been stolen, someone must have disabled the alarm system.

This, taken together with another unstated assumption:

Assumption 3: Only a member of the security firm which installed the alarm could have disabled it.

supports the:

Main conclusion: So the culprit must have been a member of the security firm which installed the alarm.

Assumptions 1 and 3 function as additional reasons. Assumption 2 functions as an intermediate conclusion.

5 The conclusion of this argument is that the few people who get measles are in greater danger than they would have been when measles was more common. Two reasons are offered as jointly supporting this claim – that many doctors have never seen a case of measles, and that the disease is difficult to diagnose without previous experience. It would not follow that measles sufferers were in *greater* danger in these circumstances if there were no effective treatments for measles.

The assumption can be stated as follows:

The complications caused by measles can be treated (with some success) if measles is diagnosed.

The assumption functions as an additional reason.

6 The argument concludes that it is carbon monoxide, rather than nicotine, which causes the higher incidence of atherosclerotic disease amongst smokers than amongst non-smokers. The evidence it gives for this is that animals exposed to carbon monoxide for several months have shown symptoms of the disease. Two assumptions are needed in order for this evidence to support the conclusion – that smoking exposes one to carbon monoxide, and that carbon monoxide affects humans and animals in the same way.

The assumptions can be stated as follows:

(a) Smokers experience higher exposure to carbon monoxide than do non-smokers.
(b) Exposure to carbon monoxide has the same effect on humans as it does on animals.

Both (a) and (b) function as additional reasons.

7 The conclusion of this argument is that reports of 'near-death' experiences are evidence that there is life after death. The reason given for this is that most of the patients who have reported experiences of this nature were neither drugged nor suffering from brain disease. This reason is offered as a rejection of the explanation by sceptics that the experiences are caused by changes in the brain which precede death, and which are similar to changes produced by drugs or brain disease. The argument relies on the assumption that these changes could occur only as a result of drugs or brain disease (which, of course, the sceptics would deny).

The assumption can be stated as follows:

The changes in the brain which produce altered states of consciousness could not occur in the absence of drugs or brain disease.

The assumption functions as an additional reason.

8 The argument concludes that the farm population in the USA has lost political power. The reason for this is that the growth of the urban population has increased the demand for food, resulting in the introduction of labour-saving technology on farms, and thus a reduction of numbers of workers engaged in farm labour and an accompanying further increase of people living and working in cities. Such changes would result in a loss of political power for the farm population only if such power depended upon the relative size of the farm population, so this must be assumed by the argument.

The assumption can be stated as follows:

The political power of the farm population is dependent upon its size relative to the rest of the population.

The assumption functions as an additional reason.

9 This argument concludes that it is important for the future of medicine to preserve wild plant species. It uses evidence from the past in order to draw this conclusion – that the progress of medicine over the past fifty years has depended upon the discovery of wonder drugs derived from wild plants. In order to draw the conclusion, it must be assumed that there are more discoveries of this kind yet to be made.

The assumption can be stated as follows:

> The development of wonder drugs from wild plants is very likely to continue in the future.

Perhaps the most natural way to fit this assumption into the argument is as an intermediate conclusion, supported by the evidence that wonder drugs have been developed from wild plants in the past.

10 This passage argues from two facts – that much larger numbers of British people are travelling abroad for holidays now than thirty years ago, and that foreign travel is expensive – to the conclusion that British people had on average less money to spend thirty years ago. This conclusion follows only if it is assumed that thirty years ago foreign travel was limited mainly or solely by the average Briton's disposable income.

The assumption can be stated as follows:

> The expense of foreign travel was the reason why the number of British people who travelled abroad for holidays was much smaller thirty years ago than it is now.

The assumption functions as an additional reason.

Exercise 8: Re-working Exercise 5

You first looked at this passage in Exercise 5, where you were asked to identify its main conclusion, and to write down a list of assumptions which you thought it made. Since this was before you read the section on identifying assumptions, you may have included some things which are not implicit reasons or implicit intermediate conclusions. You may also have missed some things which are assumptions of this kind. By comparing your answers to both Exercise 5 and Exercise 8 with the answer below, you will be able to see how much the section on identifying assumptions has helped you to understand the passage.

The first step is to identify the conclusion, which is to be found, conveniently, at the end of the passage, clearly signalled by the word 'So':

> So we must tell the snipers not to fire at Bill Clinton [because of his sex life].

Next we must look for the reasons. Each of the first three paragraphs presents a major reason, and these, taken together, are intended to support the conclusion. These reasons are quite difficult to identify, because they are wrapped up in an entertaining journalistic style. The best way to tackle this is to remember that the article is trying to convince us that there is no justification for criticizing Bill Clinton because of his sex life, and then to ask yourself,

'What major point is each paragraph attempting to make?'

The first two paragraphs aim to show that the two justifications which are usually given for examining a politician's sex life do not in fact justify criticizing Bill Clinton. The first paragraph deals with the first justification, and aims to show that this supposed justification can never be a good reason for criticizing a politician. The supposed justification is, 'if a man would cheat on his wife, he would cheat on his country.' Two lines of reasoning are offered to support the idea that this is not true – first, some examples of good husbands who were bad presidents and second, the claim that many very skilled politicians also have a high sex drive.

The second paragraph aims to show that the second justification for examining a politician's sex life does not hold good in the case of Bill Clinton. The supposed justification is that, since leaders provide examples to the nation, they are hypocritical if they 'slip from grace.' It is claimed that Bill Clinton cannot be criticized on these grounds because he has never claimed to lead an entirely decent life.

In the third paragraph, the argument tries to show that it is inconsistent to criticize Bill Clinton on the grounds of his sexual misdemeanours, whilst at the same time regarding former president John F. Kennedy, who behaved in the same way, as a great president of whom the country was robbed by his assassination.

Let's summarize what we have identified so far. The passage argues that we should not criticize Bill Clinton because of his sex life, on the grounds that:

(a) it is not true that someone who would cheat on his wife would be dishonest in his capacity as a politician,
(b) Bill Clinton does not set a bad example to the nation,
(c) it is inconsistent to criticize Bill Clinton because of his sex life whilst at the same time admiring former president John F. Kennedy.

Let us look in more detail at how these three claims are supposed to be established. The reasoning behind (a) above is as follows:

Reason 1: Gerry Ford and Jimmy Carter were, by most accounts, strong husbands but weak presidents.

Reason 2: Pat Nixon knew where Dick was every night. The problem was that the American people could not be sure where he was during the day.

These two pieces of evidence are intended to support an unstated:

Intermediate conclusion 1: Someone can be a good husband but a bad president.

There seems to be another strand of reasoning, leading from:

Reason 3: it is a sad but obvious fact that, to many of those men to whom he gave unusual political nous, God handed out too much testosterone as well.

This can be seen as meant to support an unstated:

Intermediate conclusion 2: We should expect some highly talented politicians to 'cheat on their wives.'

Intermediate conclusion 1 and Intermediate conclusion 2, taken together, are intended to support (a) above, which is also not explicitly stated. In this more detailed analysis, we shall label (a) as

Intermediate conclusion 3: It is not true that 'if a man would cheat on his wife, he would cheat on his country.'

The reasoning behind (b) above is as follows:

Reason 4: Bill Clinton, unlike many senior US politicians, has never publicly claimed that he has led an entirely decent life.

This is intended to support an unstated:

Intermediate conclusion 4: Bill Clinton is not hypocritical about sexual morality.

This, taken together with :

Reason 5: The second excuse for prurience towards rulers is that leaders, tacitly or explicitly, set examples to the nation and thus their own slips from grace are hypocritical.

is intended to support (b), which is also unstated. In this more detailed analysis, we shall label (b) as

Intermediate conclusion 5: Bill Clinton does not set a bad example to the nation.

The final paragraph describes the way in which people honour the memory of JFK, and also alludes to the stories which circulate about his sex life, which were not given publicity during his lifetime. Two claims underlie this paragraph, but are not explicitly stated. They are:

Reason 6 (unstated): Former president John F. Kennedy is widely regarded as having been a potentially great president.

Reason 7 (unstated): John F. Kennedy was guilty of sexual misdemeanours.

These two, taken together, are intended to support (c), which is also unstated. In this more detailed analysis, we shall label (c) as

Intermediate conclusion 6: It is inconsistent to criticize Bill Clinton because of his sex life whilst at the same time admiring former president John F. Kennedy.

Now let's list the unstated assumptions which this analysis identifies:

1 Someone can be a good husband but a bad president.
2 We should expect some highly talented politicians to 'cheat on their wives.'
3 It is not true that 'if a man would cheat on his wife, he would cheat on his country.'
4 Bill Clinton is not hypocritical about sexual morality.
5 Bill Clinton does not set a bad example to the nation.
6 Former president John F. Kennedy is widely regarded as having been a potentially great president.
7 Former president John F. Kennedy was guilty of sexual misdemeanours.
8 It is inconsistent to condemn Bill Clinton for his sexual misdemeanours, whilst regarding John F. Kennedy as a potentially great president.

If you have identified some of these assumptions, you may find yourself questioning the truth of them, or wondering whether they do indeed support the main conclusion. If so, you are ready to move on to the next section – Evaluating Reasoning. You may wish to look at this passage again later, and attempt to evaluate it for yourself.

Exercise 9: Identifying flaws

1 This passage asserts that a fantastic basketball team could be created, and concludes from this that the game would thereby become exciting for fans everywhere. We may doubt whether it is true that a fantastic basketball team could be created if the best player from each of the best teams formed a new club. All these 'best players' might have identical rather than complementary skills. However, we are not concerned with evaluating the truth of reasons in this exercise, so we should ask 'If it is true that a fantastic basketball team could be created if the best player from each of the best teams formed a new club, does it follow that basketball would then become an exciting game for fans everywhere? No – the evidence that a basketball team composed of extremely talented players could be created is insufficient to show that this would produce an exciting game for spectators. Perhaps it would not be exciting to watch one super-team playing against weaker opposition, and perhaps the excitement of basketball for fans depends upon seeing one's home team as having a chance of winning.

2 This is an example of the flaw of assuming that because two things have occurred together, one has caused the other. The fact that crimes have been committed when the moon is full is not a good reason to believe that the full moon causes people to commit crimes.

3 This argument draws a conclusion about one individual from evidence about what is generally true of members of the group to which that individual belongs. If we took the first sentence to mean that *every* young person today has more formal education than their grandparents had, then the conclusion about Wilma would follow. But it is more reasonable to construe the first sentence as meaning that *in general* young people today have more formal education than their grandparents had. If that is the claim, then there may be exceptions and Wilma may be one of those exceptions. Perhaps her grandparents were unusual in their generation in having a university education, and perhaps Wilma dropped out of education at an early stage.

4 The conclusion is that neither marijuana nor LSD can be harmful. The reason given for this is that doctors use them as painkillers for cancer patients. The conclusion does not follow, since doctors may have to use drugs which are harmful when the alternative – leaving the patient to suffer severe pain – is worse.

5 This passage tells us that adolescents have a higher requirement for iron than that of the rest of the population. It concludes from this that the reason why adolescents often suffer from anaemia is not that they have insufficient iron in their diets. However, if their requirement for iron is greater than normal, it is much more reasonable to conclude that their anaemia *could* be caused by insufficient iron in their diets. There is a question about the meaning of 'insufficient' in the conclusion. Adolescents suffering from anaemia may have an amount of iron in their diets which would be sufficient for all other people. But if their requirement for iron is greater, then this amount will be insufficient for them.

6 This argument concludes that if people in the West switched to a Japanese diet, then instead of dying from heart attacks, they would die from the diseases which are the most common causes of death in Japan. It bases this conclusion on two claims – that diet is an important cause of disease, and that heart attacks in the West are caused by diet. However, the evidence is insufficient to establish the conclusion, since diet may be an important cause of disease without being the only cause of disease. Hence the diseases common in Japan may be caused not by diet, but by genetic factors, or by environmental conditions. The passage does not settle the question as to what causes strokes and cancers of the stomach amongst the Japanese. So we cannot be confident that changing to a Japanese diet would increase the incidence of these diseases amongst Westerners.

7 This passage concludes that cooking must have been invented 400,000 years ago, based on the evidence that fires, which would have been necessary for cooking, were being used at that time. But the passage establishes only

that fire was *necessary* in order for cooking to be invented, not that it was *sufficient*. Perhaps the first use of fire was for warmth or to deter predators, and maybe cooking was not invented until some time later. This is an example of a common flaw – that of treating a necessary condition as if it were a sufficient condition.

8 This passage argues from the unreliability of a witness to the conclusion that what the witness said must have been false. But the evidence is insufficient for us to draw this conclusion. The most we can conclude is that Fred may not have been in the vicinity of the shop when the fire was started. Without further evidence we cannot conclude that he *must* have been somewhere else.

9 The conclusion of this argument is that most people could be musical geniuses if they practised hard enough. The evidence offered for this is that a number of composers (presumably musical geniuses) wrote their masterpieces only after a long period of training in composition. Two questionable moves have to be made in order for this evidence to be taken to support the conclusion. First it must be assumed that the practice which these composers had was *necessary* in order for them to write masterpieces. Maybe this is not too wild an assumption, but it is just possible that it was not practice, but maturity, which was required in order for them to write masterpieces. The more serious flaw is to conclude that because some people could write masterpieces as a result of practising hard, anyone could do so if they practised hard. This is to treat the necessary condition of practising or training in composition (if we concede that it is a necessary condition) as a sufficient condition for composing masterpieces. Perhaps what is also needed is a certain talent which not everyone possesses.

10 This argument concludes that there cannot be any link between being poor and committing crimes. The evidence it produces for this is that many poor people never commit a crime. But this evidence is insufficient to establish the conclusion. Even if many poor people never commit a crime, it may be true that some poor people who do commit crimes would not have done so if they had not been poor. So there could be a link between poverty and crime such that poverty makes *some* people more likely to commit crimes.

Exercise 10: Evaluating further evidence

1 The answer is (e).

(e) weakens the conclusion by giving an alternative explanation as to why those children who participate in school sports activities are less likely to fight. This alternative explanation is that those with a tendency to fight are not allowed to participate in school sports activities.

(a) has no impact on the conclusion. The supervision by adults of sports activities at school may explain why there was little fighting during sports. But the conclusion is about why those who participate in sports are less likely to fight at any time during school hours, and not just during sports activities.

(b) does not weaken the conclusion, since even if the participants in school sports activities are discouraged from being extremely aggressive, the physical activity of sport may be such as to channel aggressive energy into non-aggressive competition.

(c) at first sight looks as if it is contradicting the statement that children who do not participate in sports fight more than those who do. So you may have been tempted to pick (c). But 'tend to be more aggressive physically' does not mean 'tend to fight more.' It means 'have a greater underlying tendency towards aggression.' If this were true, and it were also true that these children fight less, this would strengthen the conclusion that participation in sport is channelling physical aggression which might otherwise be released through fighting.

(d) is irrelevant to the conclusion. The time during the school day at which fights usually occur makes no difference to the explanation as to why those who do not participate in school sports activities are more likely to fight.

2 The answer is (d).

(d) weakens the argument by showing that if businesses did what is recommended – that is, reduced salaries for employees without advanced engineering degrees – this could eventually be to the disadvantage of engineering businesses. Although it might have the desirable effect of persuading more engineering graduates to take PhDs (and thereby increase the numbers of engineering teachers), it might also result in fewer enrolments of students on undergraduate engineering courses. In the long term this could lead to a shortage of good applicants for jobs in engineering, which would be against the interests of businesses.

(a) is irrelevant to the conclusion. If 'the sciences' do not include engineering, then (a) is not even on the same topic as the argument. If 'the sciences' do include engineering, then (a) adds nothing to the information in the passage that enrolment in engineering courses has increased.

(b) does not weaken the argument. It simply emphasizes the problem – the need to attract more engineers into teaching – to which the argument offers a solution.

(c) has no impact on the argument. The high salaries paid by businesses to those with advanced engineering degrees are likely to tempt these people away from teaching. This makes no difference to the recommendation to solve the problem of the shortage of engineering teachers by reducing salaries for those without advanced degrees.

(e) has no impact on the argument. The argument is about a way of increasing the incentive for engineering graduates to pursue postgraduate studies. The funding of research programmes would not increase this incentive, unless it made generous awards to potential students. (e) makes no claim that businesses fund generous awards to students.

3 The answer is (e).

(e) strengthens Joan's claim by providing evidence that some heroin addicts are likely to commit serious crimes in order to get supplies of the drug. This supports the claim that the amount of serious crime might be reduced if heroin addicts were given free supplies of the drug.

(a) does not strengthen Joan's claim, it weakens it. If heroin addicts were more likely to be violent when under the influence of heroin, they might commit crimes at such times. Providing them with free heroin would not reduce the amount of crime, if any, committed by heroin addicts.

(b) does not strengthen Joan's claim, because she is not trying to show that supplying heroin to addicts would make economic sense. She is claiming simply that it would reduce crime.

(c) does not strengthen Joan's claim, for the same reason that (b) does not strengthen it.

(d) does not strengthen Joan's claim because it concerns crime which is not related to the use of heroin. This tells us nothing about the effectiveness of Joan's proposed method of reducing drug-related crime.

4 The answer is (a).

If (a) is true, then there is a good reason for the automobile association to continue testing direction indicators, since if they do not, the numbers of defective direction indicators may increase. Hence (a) weakens the case for stopping inspection of direction indicators.

(b) on its own does not weaken the argument. It seems to offer a reason for making sure that direction indicators are in good working order. But this does not weaken the recommendation to stop inspecting them, unless – as (a) suggests – stopping the inspections would result in more faulty indicators.

(c) does not weaken the recommendation, unless there is reason to believe that the inspection procedures need to be as thorough as those in neighbouring states. (c) does not provide such a reason.

(d) does not weaken the recommendation to stop testing direction indicators. It appears to be offering a reason in support of the recommendation, but in fact it makes no difference either way. Even if automobiles fail the inspection on the grounds of other safety defects, there may still be automobiles with defective indicators on the roads.

(e) does not weaken the argument, although it may look as if it is offering a reason for retaining inspection of indicators. Inspecting them would not bring to light other defects not covered by the safety inspection system. So (e) is irrelevant to the question as to whether direction indicators should be inspected.

5 The answer is (d).

The researchers concluded that if parents monitored (presumably meaning 'controlled') the amount of time which their children spent watching television, the children's performance in school would benefit. So the researchers were assuming that the relationship they found between the hours the children spent watching television and their level of performance in school was evidence that watching for longer periods *caused* poorer performance. The researchers had discovered a correlation, but a correlation between two things does not necessarily mean that one thing causes the other (see the discussion on pp. 47–8). Statement (d) strengthens the idea that there is a causal connection. If differences in performance are less when hours watching television are roughly the same for all children, then it is likely that differences in time spent watching television cause differences in performance.

(a) gives more detail about the figures upon which the claim in the first sentence is based, so it strengthens the statement that if children watched between two and three hours of television per day, they were likely to perform less well in school. This is stronger evidence that there is a correlation, but gives no extra evidence of a causal connection. So it does not strengthen the conclusion, which relies on the assumption that there is a causal connection.

Provided we assume that there is a causal connection between amount of television viewing and school performance, (b) could be regarded as giving an additional reason why school performance might improve if parents monitored their children's television viewing. But since (b) does nothing to strengthen the idea that there is a causal connection, it does not strengthen the conclusion of the researchers.

(c) does not strengthen the idea that watching television for two or more hours per day causes poorer performance in school. Instead it introduces a new factor – the amount of time spent reading – which may have an effect on school performance.

(e) does not strengthen the idea of a causal connection, because although it suggests that some children replaced their television watching with reading, it does not comment upon how this affected their performance in school.

6 The answer is (a).

(a) weakens the argument by showing that even if ex-prisoners do not pursue the occupation for which they have prepared whilst in prison, the skills they have learnt during training in prison may nevertheless be of use in whatever occupation they take up.
(b) provides an *objection* to scrapping career training programmes in prison. But this is not the same as weakening the argument, because it has no impact on the claim that it is *unwise* to continue such programmes since they do not achieve their aims.
(c) mentions an advantage of prison career training programmes, thereby to some extent weakening the claim that it is unwise to continue them. But this does not weaken the argument as much as (a), which shows that the claim upon which the conclusion of the argument is based – that the programmes do not achieve their aim (which we can assume is to provide skills which will be useful in future employment) – is not true.
(d) does not weaken the argument, because it simply emphasizes that training programmes have the goal which the argument claims they do not achieve. (d) tells us nothing about whether they achieve that goal, hence has no impact on the conclusion that these programmes should be scrapped.
(e) does not weaken the argument, because the argument relies on the claim that prisoners choose not to pursue the occupation for which they have trained whilst in prison. This does not imply that they have no choice whilst in prison, nor does (e) imply that they will not change their choice of occupation after leaving prison.

7 The answer is (e).

(e) weakens the argument by providing evidence that the physiological changes recorded by a lie detector may result from stress other than the stress caused by lying. This suggests that, contrary to what the conclusion claims, reliable lie detection is not possible.
(a) has no impact on the argument, because reliable lie detection may be possible, even if the machines are expensive and require careful maintenance.
(b) suggests that for some people who are lying, lie detectors will indicate symptoms of only moderate stress. But this does not weaken the claim that reliable lie detection is possible.

(c) does not weaken the argument, because it does not suggest that it is impossible to find and train the personnel who can use lie detection instruments effectively.
(d) does not weaken the argument, because reliable lie detection may be possible even if some people misuse or abuse lie detecting equipment.

Exercise 11: Offering alternative explanations

These answers identify the fact and the explanation offered in each passage. They then give one or more possible alternative explanations. You may be able to think of other possible explanations.

1
- *Fact:* Public confidence in the police force is declining at the same time as fear of crime is growing.
- *Explanation:* Fear of crime is caused by lack of confidence in the police.
- *Alternative explanation:* Fear of crime is caused by people's belief that the incidence of crime is increasing.

2
- *Fact:* The divorce rate has increased greatly over the last thirty years.
- *Explanation:* There are more unhappy marriages than there used to be.
- *Alternative explanation:* It is now easier to obtain a divorce, and the stigma associated with divorce has gone. (Hence there may have been just the same percentage of unhappy marriages in the past, but people did not divorce because it was difficult or because others would disapprove.)

3
- *Fact:* The human race has never received a well-authenticated communication from beings elsewhere in the universe.
- *Explanation:* The only intelligent life in the universe is on our planet.
- *Alternative explanations:* There is intelligent life elsewhere in the universe and
  - they don't want to communicate with us, or
  - they don't know we are here, or
  - we have failed to recognize their communications.

4
- *Fact:* Whenever a new road is built, the density of traffic in that area increases.
- *Explanation:* The number of cars per head of population is increasing.
- *Alternative explanation:* When new roads are built, the average number of journeys per motorist increases (i.e. when roads are better, people have more incentive to drive).

5
- *Fact:* The number of people taking holidays in British resorts declined last summer.
- *Explanation:* The weather was bad in Britain last summer.
- *Alternative explanations:*

- For financial reasons fewer people took holidays.
- Prices for holidays abroad were reduced.
- There was bad publicity about pollution on British beaches.

Exercise 12: Identifying and evaluating explanations

Each of these answers identifies the fact or facts for which explanations are offered, identifies the possible explanations offered in the text, and suggests some other possible explanations. You may have thought up different possible explanations. We leave you to draw your own conclusions as to which explanation is the most plausible.

1 (a) *Fact:* Girls perform better than boys in GCSE exams.

(b) *Explanations in text:*
- Girls have clearer goals and are more focused – boys have no idea what they want to do after GCSE.
- Boys do not want to appear swotty – study is not seen as bad for girls' image.
- Boys get less attention from teachers than girls do.

(c) *Other possible explanations* (some suggested by comments in text):
- Teachers' lower expectations of boys' abilities cause boys to perform less well than they could.
- Boys are unable to concentrate or organize themselves, and lack motivation.
- Girls are cleverer than boys.
- Girls work harder than boys.
- Girls reach intellectual maturity earlier than boys.

2 In this example there are several facts for which explanations are offered.

(a) *Fact:* Fewer people were killed on Britain's roads last year than in any year since 1926.

(b) *Explanations in text:*
- There is better paramedic treatment at the roadside and better medical care.
- The figures are misleading because deaths which occur as a result of road accidents are counted as road deaths only if the death occurs within 30 days of the accident, and now people are kept alive longer by modern medical techniques.
- There has been a decline in the numbers of vulnerable road users such as pedestrians and cyclists.

(c) *Other possible explanations:*
- Roads are safer, due to better road construction, and/or safer driving.

- Cars are safer for their occupants, due to seat-belts, air-bags, crumple zones, side-impact bars, better brakes and so on.

(a) *Fact:* Child casualties are proportionally higher in Britain than in other European countries.
(b) *Explanation in text:* Children in Britain have to walk home from school in the dark in winter.
(c) *Other possible explanation:*
There are more child pedestrians in areas of heavy traffic in Britain than in other European countries.

(a) *Fact:* The number of children killed on the roads and the number of serious injuries on the roads have both increased.
(b) *Explanations in text:*
- Roads are more dangerous.
- Drivers make mistakes because they feel too insulated in modern cars.

(c) *Other possible explanation:*
There is more traffic on the roads.

3 (a) *Fact:* A statue of the Virgin Mary has been observed to appear to shed tears.
(b) *Explanation in text:* It is likely that the statue is made of permeable material with an impermeable glaze, and that it has a hollow centre. If the glaze over the eyes is scratched, droplets of water appear, and it looks as if the statue is weeping.
(c) *Other possible explanation:* The statue is weeping, and this is a miracle.

With this example you may find it impossible to think up any further possible explanations, but you should have a lively discussion as to which of these is more plausible, and how you might find out.

Exercise 13: Practising the skills

1

1 *Conclusions:* Although it is clear that reasoning is going on in this passage, it is difficult to identify a firm main conclusion. It is examining the case for a recommendation to allow drivers on British motorways to pass other cars on the left as well as on the right, but does not come out with a firm decision about this. The conclusion on this topic, though not directly stated, seems to be that we should not yet allow 'undertaking' on British motorways.

In the last paragraph there is a recommendation as to what should be done whilst further evidence is being sought. So we could say that the passage offers a second conclusion that 'in the meantime, safety would be improved by a change to the Highway Code obliging drivers not only to indicate before changing lanes, but also to leave their indicators on while they are in the overtaking lane.'

2 *Reasons/assumptions:* The reason for the first conclusion is that 'there is little evidence either way' as to whether it would be a good thing to allow 'undertaking.' The reasons offered in support of this intermediate conclusion are that overtaking on both sides works well in the USA, and British traffic conditions have come more and more to resemble those of the USA; but British conditions are different in some respects which may be important (higher speeds and narrower roads), and British drivers may not adjust well to the change.

The reason offered in support of the second conclusion is that 'the flashing indicator would serve as an unaggressive signal to drivers in front to pull over to the left as quickly as they safely can; and it would remind the overtaker to do the same immediately afterwards.' The second conclusion relies also on an assumption that a change to the Highway Code obliging drivers to leave their indicators flashing whilst they are in the overtaking lane would be generally observed.

3 *Assessing reasons/assumptions:* The truth of the claim that the system of overtaking on both sides works well in the USA could be established by examining accident statistics in the USA – checking whether accidents on freeways are frequently caused by lane changing. The comments about British conditions are very tentative – in fact they are posed as questions, rather than stated as truths. So we merely have to accept that traffic conditions might be so different in Britain as to cause problems.

It is difficult to assess the truth of the claim that a flashing indicator whilst in the overtaking lane would be an unaggressive reminder to other drivers, and would remind the overtaker to pull over. We can each think about what our own reactions would be to such a signal, but the decisive test would be whether such signals, if widely used, changed drivers' behaviour.

The assumption that drivers would observe the directive – to keep their indicator flashing is very dubious, especially in view of the fact which causes the whole problem – that many drivers ignore the directive to return after overtaking to the lane from which they came.

4 *Authorities cited:* No specific sources of evidence are mentioned. The passage recommends consultation with experts, but does not say who these experts are (though it clearly doesn't regard the Automobile Association as 'expert'!).

5 *Further evidence:* For this question, you have to think about any knowledge which you have which strengthens or weakens the conclusion.

6 *Explanations:* The passage does not contain any obvious explanations.

7 *Flawed reasoning:* The intermediate conclusion, that there is little evidence either way, is not firmly established by the reasons. We need to know whether there are any countries with traffic conditions similar to Britain in which overtaking on both sides works well. We need to know whether traffic experts in Britain have attempted to simulate the conditions for overtaking on both sides. If it is true that there is as yet little evidence either way, then perhaps it is sensible not to make a change until further evidence is available.
We should have reservations about accepting the second conclusion, since, as stated above, the assumption that drivers would observe the directive to leave their indicators on whilst overtaking is questionable.

2

1 *Conclusion:* The main message of the passage is that lowering the price of a product can not only persuade people to buy your brand as opposed to another brand, but can actually increase consumption of the type of product. For example, lowering the price of *The Times*, it is suggested, not only persuaded some people to buy *The Times* as opposed to other newspapers, but also persuaded some people who would not otherwise have bought a newspaper to buy *The Times*, and some people to buy *The Times* in addition to their regular newspaper.

The conclusion is stated in a number of places:

> If you lower your prices, it is very likely that you will *enlarge* the market for your sort of product. *(paragraph one)*
>
> lowering prices by cutting profit margins to the bone can do more than merely redistribute a fixed amount of custom, by actually enticing more people into a market they might otherwise not enter at all. *(paragraph two)*
>
> cut prices as low as you can and people will buy more *(paragraph four)*

Although not explicitly stated as a conclusion, there is a hint that it is possible to lower prices *and maintain the same level of profit*, by increasing the volume of sales though lowering the amount of profit per item sold.

2 *Reasons/assumptions:* The immediate reasons for the conclusion are that 'people's tastes and preferences are not immutable' and 'they will exercise their freedom to choose when given half an economic chance.' Some support is given for the claim that people will exercise freedom to choose by offering examples of people choosing to buy less of a product (cigarettes, and meals in restaurants) when prices go up.

Further support is offered by the example of increased sales of *The Times*, by the prevailing philosophy in the United States of running on low profit margins, and by Tesco's report that both sales and profits were up as a result of a lower pricing policy.

3 *Assessing reasons/assumptions:* It seems reasonable to accept that people can change their tastes and habits of consumption, and that price changes – both up and down – can influence their inclination to buy a certain type of product.

4 *Authorities cited:* There is no reason to doubt the reliability of the report from Tesco.

5 *Further evidence:* You have to consider whether you have any knowledge which strengthens or weakens the conclusion.

6 *Explanations*: There are no obvious explanations in the passage.

7 *Flawed reasoning:* There are three problems with this argument, all concerned with exactly what the scope of the conclusion is. The conclusion seems to be a very general claim that, *whatever your product*, lowering prices is likely to enlarge the market for your sort of product. If the claims about increased sales of *The Times* are true – that more people started buying newspapers as a result of the reduction in price – then this shows that at least for some products a reduction in price can enlarge the market. But perhaps this is not true for all products. There must, for example, be a limit to the amount of food people consume, regardless of how low prices drop. Some of the examples do not really give support to the general claim that lower prices will enlarge markets. One example tells us that when cigarette prices increase, the number of people smoking drops. It does not follow from this that if cigarette prices fell more people would start smoking. The example of Tesco shows only that lowering prices can increase *one* supermarket's sales. It does not follow that there was an increase in the market for supermarket merchandise. Perhaps the new customers at Tesco had defected from other supermarkets.

The second problem concerns whether we are intended to conclude that a producer or a retailer can *at any given time* increase sales by lowering prices. But this would have an absurd implication. Taken to its logical conclusion, it would mean that one could go on and on and on reducing prices and increasing sales. A point would come at which the product cost nothing, and the retailer was not making sales at all, but was giving the product away. However, since the author appears to be recommending 'lowering prices by cutting profit margins to the bone', it seems that she is not recommending that it is always sensible to lower prices in order to increase sales. She would not regard it as sensible to do so if this would result in no profit at all.

The final problem concerns whether we are intended to conclude that it is possible for all businesses in an economy to lower prices and increase profit. The example of supermarkets in the United States seems to suggest that it is possible to have very low profit margins, and still run a profitable business. But perhaps this is possible only with very large scale businesses. And perhaps it is possible only if competitors frequently go out of business. Neither the United States example nor the Tesco example shows that you can enlarge the market by lowering prices; thus, although they show that some businesses can increase profits whilst lowering prices, they do not show that all businesses can do this.

3

1 Conclusion: The conclusion appears in the last paragraph, where we can see that the main point is being made, summing up what can (or cannot) be concluded from the evidence previously presented. The conclusion is that the evidence does not support the assumption that the incidence of violent and serious crimes has increased greatly over the past forty to fifty years.

2 Reasons/assumptions: The reasons offered are, in the first paragraph, that only 5 per cent of crimes are violent, and that in some categories where there has been an increase in figures, much of the crime is trivial and to do with increased opportunity for theft and vandalism; in the second paragraph, that people are more inclined to report crime now than they used to be, which accounts for the rise in reported crime; in the third paragraph that theft and violence were commonplace in the Thirties in London.

In the second paragraph, there is an assumption that in the past, both domestic physical violence and rape by intimates and acquaintances happened, but tended not to be reported.

3 Assessing reasons/assumptions: In order to know the truth of some of the reasons, for example, whether much of the crime in categories where reported crime has increased is trivial, we would have to check statistics on crime. But for those reasons which concern the level of criminal activity in the past which did not get reported, establishing truth or falsity seems difficult. We could read historical accounts of life in the Thirties. But it is quite possible that the assumption that there used to be much domestic physical violence which was never reported is true, even if there is no evidence of it in historical records.

4 Authorities cited: Sources of evidence are not given in the passage. Presumably the figures quoted come from official statistics on crime.

5 Further Evidence: This is a question about any knowledge of your own which strengthens or weakens the conclusion.

6 Explanations: The passage gives two explanations to account for at least some of the rise in crime figures. First, some of the increase in burglaries and vandalism is claimed to be attributable to the fact that there are more things to steal and vandalize. Second, the increase in reported crime is attributed to an increasing tendency to report crimes, rather than an increase in crimes committed. These are being presented as alternatives to the assumption that the rise in recorded crime is attributable to an increasing tendency amongst some of the population to commit violent and serious crimes. In the absence of further evidence, the explanations offered in the passage are as plausible as is the assumption which they seek to overturn.

7 *Flawed reasoning:* The conclusion is that the evidence available does not support the assumption that the incidence of violent and serious crimes has increased greatly over the past forty to fifty years. By offering another plausible explanation for the increase in *reported* crime, the argument supports this conclusion quite well. Of course, if the author wanted to conclude that violent and serious crime definitely has not increased, more evidence would be needed.

Exercise 14: Drawing conclusions

1 The temperature must have dropped to below freezing point overnight.
2 It is likely that Gitta has 'flu.
3 The daffodils will probably flower late this year.
4 Jane's car must have travelled faster than Jim's.
5 If Ms Brown killed the murder victim, she must have poisoned him.

Exercise 15: Assessing implications

1 (a) *Probably false:* The passage states that the incidence of skin cancer is higher amongst professionals than amongst manual workers, which suggests that there are some cases amongst manual workers.

(b) *Insufficient information:* If 20 per cent of cases occur amongst those aged 20 to 39, and 80 per cent amongst over-forties (though it may be less than 80 per cent, because some cases may occur amongst under-twenties), it looks more likely that the risk is greater for over-forties. But we do not have enough information to conclude that (b) is false, first because it makes a general claim, and we have figures only about the incidence in Sweden, and second because we do not know about any differences in lifestyles of the two age groups in Sweden which may account for the greater percentage of cases amongst the over-forties.

(c) *False:* The increased incidence of skin cancer in Sweden could be caused by exposure to sunlight, since more people from Sweden may be taking holidays in sunny countries. Of course, it may be true that exposure to sunlight is not the only cause of skin cancer, but it is false that the figures from Sweden indicate this.

(d) *Insufficient information:* Although we are told that only 20 per cent of cases occur in the 20 to 39 age group, and that exposure to sunlight is a significant cause of skin cancer, we do not know whether the higher number of cases amongst over-forties is attributable to greater exposure to sunlight for this group, or to a greater tendency for older people to succumb to skin cancer, even given equal exposure to that of younger people.

(e) *True:* We can conclude that the increased incidence of skin cancer in Sweden *may* be due to an increase in numbers holidaying in sunny countries. In answering 'true' to (e), we are not concluding that this is the cause. (e) merely states tentatively that it may be.

2 (a) *Insufficient information:* We are told only about the sample of 600 drivers. Even if most of them had an inflated sense of their own safety as car drivers, this information cannot support the claim that most drivers have an inflated sense of their safety. The drivers in this sample may not have been representative of drivers in general. They may have been chosen because of their unusual attitudes.

(b) *Probably true:* If most of the group overestimate their driving skills, then some of the 50 per cent who said they would drive at over 80 mph on a motorway must also overestimate their driving skills. Assuming that 80 mph is too fast, and that the drivers do as they say, then these drivers tend to drive too fast on motorways. Since these assumptions are not unreasonable, it is probably true that some drivers who overestimate their skills tend to drive too fast.

(c) *Probably false:* We are told that those most likely to overestimate their driving skills are young men. Since young men are likely to have had only a few years' driving experience, it is probably false that those with only a few years' driving experience do not overestimate their driving skills.

(d) *True:* The study demonstrated that forcing drivers to imagine that they had caused a serious accident made some of them change their judgement about the speed at which they would be prepared to drive. Assuming that the effect on their attitudes is long-term, and that they act in accordance with this changed judgement, some of them will drive more responsibly, with respect to speed, in the future. So it is true that imagining the accident may make them drive more responsibly in the future.

(e) *Insufficient information:* We are told that the drivers were asked to *imagine* the lack of confidence they might experience if they caused a serious accident. But this does not imply that they actually lost confidence in their driving as a result.

3 (a) *False:* because although a change in personality may be a symptom of a brain tumour, there may be other causes of a change in personality.
(b) *Insufficient information:* We are told that a brain scan can diagnose a tumour, but we are not told whether there are or are not any adverse effects of a brain scan.
(c) *Probably false:* We are told that neurologists think that a headache which has persisted for a year with no other symptoms is unlikely to be due to a tumour. But since it is also stated that headaches are amongst the symptoms of brain tumours, then it is very probable that neurologists, who are experts in brain diseases, believe that headaches are sometimes symptoms of tumours.
(d) *True:* The earliest symptoms of a brain tumour are headaches, vomiting and failing vision. If someone has these symptoms, then it would be sensible to find out as soon as possible whether there is a brain tumour, since the earlier a diagnosis is made, the better the chances that treatment will be successful. Since a brain scan can diagnose a tumour, it would be a good idea to have a brain scan.
(e) *True:* All the symptoms mentioned here have, we are told, other possible causes. So someone could have all these symptoms without having a brain tumour.

4 (a) *Probably true:* Although the passage refers to a ewe forming a bond with 'its own lamb', this use of the singular noun does not suggest that a ewe can form a bond with only one of its own lambs. The statement that the ewe 'rejects all others' is best understood as meaning that she rejects all except her own lambs.
(b) *Insufficient information, or Probably false?* Strictly speaking we do not have enough information in this passage to conclude either that a ewe will or that she will not reject her own lamb if she is introduced to another lamb. However, given a few assumptions, we can conclude that (b) is probably false. First, if the ewe really believes she has given birth to another lamb, then presumably she can form bonds with both her own and the orphaned lamb in the same way that she could (we have assumed above) form bonds with both her own twin lambs. Second, unless the farmers are using this technique only with ewes whose own lambs have died shortly after birth, there would be no point in using the technique at all if it resulted in an orphaned lamb being accepted by the foster mother, whilst her own lamb was rejected.
(c) *True:* We are told that lack of maternal contact can cause behaviour abnormalities.
(d) *False:* We are told that farmers do rear orphaned lambs themselves. Such lambs may have behaviour abnormalities, but can nevertheless grow to adulthood.

(e) *True:* There is an 80 per cent chance of a ewe accepting, and thus of forming a bond with, an orphaned lamb, if the farmer uses the technique of fooling the ewe into thinking she has given birth to another lamb.

5 (a) *Insufficient information:* The passage makes it clear that scab and blowfly attacks cause damage to sheepskins. This may be sufficient reason for farmers to want to use sheep dip. Without further information, we cannot tell whether these parasites cause distress to sheep.

(b) *False:* There is some evidence of a possible link in 58 of the cases examined.

(c) *Insufficient information:* Three of the people whose symptoms may have been caused by using sheep dip were wearing protective clothing. If these three people's symptoms were definitely caused by using sheep dip, then we could conclude that the clothing does not prevent damage to health when using sheep dip, and thus that (c) is false. But we do not know whether their symptoms were definitely caused by the use of the sheep dip.

(d) *False:* We are told that it is not known what the effects of exposure to sheep dip are. Even though we must conclude that (d) is false, this is not the same as saying that there is no justification for banning the use of sheep dip. Some people might argue that if there is any potential risk to health, its use should be banned.

(e) *Probably true:* There is some evidence of a potential risk, and the Ministry of Agriculture is sufficiently concerned to ensure that sheep dips are handled only by those with a certificate of competence.

Exercise 16: Identifying parallel arguments

1 The answer is (d). They both have the following structure:

Because Xs usually have characteristic Y, and
because Z has characteristic Y, it follows that
Z is probably an X.

In the original argument,

X = heroin addict
Y = needle marks on their arms
Z = Robert

In (d),

X = students
Y = age of less than 25 years
Z = Harold

The structure of (a) is:
Because Xs usually have Y, and
because Z is an X,
Z probably has Y.

The structure of (b) is:
Because patients with X usually have Y,
X probably causes Y.

The structure of (c) is:
Because Xs have Y, and
because people with Y do Z,
Xs probably do Z.

The structure of (e) is:
Because Xs usually have characteristic Y,
most Xs probably do Z.

2 The answer is (b). The last sentence and (b) both reason as follows:
X did (does) not cause Y,
Y caused (causes) X.

In the original passage,
X = high infant mortality
Y = the indifference of parents towards their children

In (b),
X = lack of qualified workers in the poor sectors of an economy
Y = low wages

The structure of (a) is:
It was not X which caused Y,
it was Z which caused Y.

The structure of (c) is:
X does not cause Y,
Y happens whether X happens or not.

The structure of (d) is:
If X does Z, it harms X and Y.

The structure of (e) is:
It was not considered worthy for Xs to do Y,
but many Xs did Y.

3 The answer is (a). (a) and the passage both have the following underlying structure:
In one case (or in some cases), the absence of X has not prevented the occurrence of disastrous result Y.
Therefore, X does not have the disastrous results which it is supposed to have.

In the original passage,

X = rapid population growth
Y = political and economic decline

In (a),

X = smoking cigarettes
Y = chronic respiratory illnesses

(b) starts with a statement which could be seen as similar in structure to the first statement of the original passage:

Using expensive paint (the absence of cheap paint) did not remove the need to apply two coats (did not prevent the disastrous result of having to apply two coats).

But the conclusion of (b) makes no reference to cheap paint not having the disastrous results it is supposed to have.

(c) could also be seen as starting off in a similar way to the passage:

Using less energy (the absence of high energy consumption) will not prevent an increase in oil imports.
But there is no suggestion that using less energy has been claimed to have disastrous results.

Neither (d) nor (e) even begins with a similar structure to the original passage. (d) begins with:

X causes Y for some Z.

(e) begins with:

Some X are Y and Z.

Exercise 17: Applying and evaluating principles

Here are some suggested applications of the principles. You may have thought of different applications, so don't regard these suggestions as the only 'right' answers.

1 People who never travel by public transport should not have to pay that portion of taxes which subsidizes public transport.
2 We should not have laws which prevent people from engaging in dangerous sports, or which require people to take safety precautions when they take part in dangerous activities. (There is a problem in applying this principle, because of vagueness in the phrase 'harm others.' It is quite difficult to think of harm to one person which would have no impact on others – for example serious injury to a mountaineer is likely to cause some suffering to their family.)

3 Newspapers should be allowed to publish views which are insulting and offensive to particular groups or individuals.
4 Doctors should tell patients the truth about the seriousness of their illnesses, or about the risks involved in operations.
5 Suppose a friend has confessed to you that they were involved in a crime, and you have promised to tell no-one. You then find out that someone else is likely to go to prison for this crime, and that, apart from your friend, you are the only person who knows they are the culprit. This principle tells you that you should tell no one else the truth.

Exercise 18: Clarifying words or phrases

1 This argument concludes that in order to be beautiful, you only have to be *average*, rather than unusual. The evidence for this claim comes from an experiment in which pictures of faces which had been made up of parts of a number of individual faces were generally judged to be more attractive than any genuine individual face.

The word which needs clarification here is *average*. The composite faces in the experiment could be said to be average in the sense of being a sum of little bits of different people's faces (for example, the length of a nose might have been determined by adding up the lengths of 16 different noses and dividing by 16). But the conclusion contrasts being average with being unusual, which suggests that here 'average' is being taken to mean 'typical.' Someone whose face has the 'average' dimensions of the composite faces in the experiment may not be 'average' in the sense of being typical. Such a person may be very unusual.

2 This passage concludes that *empathy* is a necessary but not a sufficient characteristic for being a good citizen. The example used to show that empathy is necessary in order to be a good citizen is of people who lack empathy in the sense of lacking concern about the suffering of others.

But the example used to show that empathy is insufficient for being a good citizen (the businessman who understands the feelings of others, and uses this understanding to exploit them) appears to *define* empathy as understanding the feelings of others, rather than caring about the suffering of others. If empathy means merely understanding the feelings of others, then empathy is not sufficient for being a good citizen. But if empathy means both understanding and caring about the feelings and sufferings of others, then empathy is a good basis for being a good citizen.

3 This passage recommends that doctors should be *honest* with their patients, for two reasons:

- telling lies can lead to a breakdown of trust, and
- patients have a right to know everything about their medical condition.

This second reason is also used to support the claim that those patients who ask about their condition should be given truthful answers to their questions. This could be taken to suggest both that patients who do not ask about their condition do not need to be told, and that those who do ask do not need to be given more information than is included in truthful answers to their direct questions.

But being *honest* could be construed not just as 'not telling lies', but as 'giving all the information one has.' The second reason itself – that patients have a right to know everything about their medical condition – seems to support this second interpretation of 'being honest.' If doctors are to be told to 'be honest' with their patients, it has to be clear whether this means simply 'never tell lies to patients' or 'give full information to patients, whether they ask or not.'

Exercise 19: Writing a summary

In each of these answers a brief summary is given with which your summary can be compared. However, your summary can be a good one even if it does not exactly match the example, since you were asked to express the summary in your own words.

1 This passage is trying to convince me that awarding more generous damages to victims of medical negligence will not result in doctors giving treatment which is not tailored to the needs of patients, on the grounds that:

- doctors are more likely to avoid litigation if they tailor treatment to the needs of patients,
- doctors themselves do not pay the compensation,
- knowing that patients can sue for negligence may make doctors more careful.

The first of these three reasons is supported by the information that the decision as to whether medical negligence has occurred is judged against the standard of a 'reasonably competent doctor' – a standard set by the medical profession, which must, therefore, be primarily concerned with whether the doctor has tailored treatment to the needs of the patient.

The second of the above reasons is supported by the claim that most medical accidents occur in hospitals, and payment of damages for such cases is the responsibility of health authorities, not of doctors.

2 This passage is trying to get me to accept that the results of IQ tests taken at an early age cannot be used to indicate future success in life, on the grounds that:

- measures of ability are not reliable unless they are collected at different points in an individual's life,
- IQ tests cannot distinguish between the top few per cent,
- there are other influences on success in addition to intelligence (such as opportunity, the will to strive, socioeconomic status, gender).

Support is offered for the first of these reasons from the examples of Freud, Einstein and Picasso. Some evidence is offered to support the third of these reasons from the Terman studies, and the example of young Asians in America.

3 This passage is trying to persuade me that teenagers should be provided with the sex education and contraception they need to take control of their reproductive health, on the grounds that the next generation of children will be healthier if mothers can choose not to become pregnant until they are mature.

This reason is supported by the claim that, even for teenagers who are well nourished and have good quality medical care during pregnancy, their babies are much more likely to be premature and undersized than the babies of older mothers. The explanation offered for this is that teenagers have not finished growing, and thus the mother and the foetus may be competing for nutrients.

Exercise 20: Ten longer passages to evaluate

For this exercise, answers are provided for only three passages – numbers 1, 8, and 9. Each answer gives one possible analysis of the passage – your analysis may differ and yet be a good analysis. Your evaluation of the passage may also differ, because some of these issues are topical, and when you do your evaluation, you may be aware of new evidence which has come to light.

Passage 1

1 *Conclusion and reasons:* The passage is trying to get us to accept that the incessant crying of some babies during the first three months of life is not due to 'colic', but is due to distress caused by nervousness and anxiety in the mother. The reasons given for this are:

- 'colic' crying ceases, as if by magic, around the third or fourth month of life . . . at just the point where the baby is beginning to be able to identify its mother as a known individual;

- mothers with cry-babies are tentative, nervous and anxious in their dealings with their offspring, whereas mothers with quieter infants are deliberate, calm and serene; and
- babies are acutely aware of differences in tactile 'security' and 'safety', on the one hand, and tactile 'insecurity' and 'alarm' on the other.

2 *Assumptions:* There are two assumptions relating to explanations. The assumption which must be added to the first reason above is that the correct explanation of the baby's ceasing to cry at three months is that a bond has been formed with the mother. The assumption which must be added to the second reason above is that the correct explanation of the connection between babies' crying on the one hand and mothers' nervousness and anxiety on the other is that the anxiety of the mother causes the baby to cry.

3 *Assessing reasons/assumptions:* Is it true that so-called 'colic' crying ceases at three months? Many mothers with 'cry-babies' would confirm this. Is it true that three months is the age at which babies form a bond with the mother? Since the baby cannot be asked about its feelings, we have to judge this from the baby's behaviour. Psychologists observe behaviour such as eye contact, smiling at a familiar face, distress when a familiar person goes away. Many psychologists accept that the process of forming attachments to mothers is gradual, but there is some evidence of it as early as three months.

Is it true that mothers with babies who cry a lot are anxious, whereas those with quieter babies are calm? Although the passage does not explicitly say that observations of a sample of mothers have been done, it seems to suggest that this is so. If such studies have not been done, they could be done and, provided a large and representative sample of mothers were chosen, they could provide strong evidence for or against this claim.

Is it true that babies are aware of differences in tactile 'security' and 'safety', on the one hand, and tactile 'insecurity' and 'alarm' on the other? Again, this can only be concluded from observation of their behaviour, and in order to evaluate the truth of the claim, we should look at any evidence which psychologists have produced. Both the assumptions we identified were to do with explanations, so we will consider their plausibility under 6 below.

4 *Authorities cited:* The passage does not refer to any authorities, but in order to evaluate the truth of the reasons, we would perhaps have to rely on the authority of psychologists who had observed the behaviour of babies.

5 *Further evidence:* Did you think of any additional information which would strengthen or weaken the conclusion?

6 *Explanations:* We identified two explanations. The first was that the

cessation of the baby's crying at three months is due to the formation of a bond between mother and infant. Even if we found good evidence of the formation of such a bond, it would not follow that the bond caused the cessation of crying. Another possible explanation for the cessation of crying is that some young babies do indeed have a physical problem, and that they cry because they are in pain. This is what is usually assumed by those who refer to the problem as 'colic.' They assume that the digestive system of some very young babies may produce a great deal of wind which can cause pain, but that such problems disappear as the baby grows.

The second explanation was of the fact that mothers with cry-babies are tentative, nervous and anxious in their dealings with their offspring, whereas mothers with quieter infants are deliberate, calm and serene. The explanation taken for granted was that the mother's anxiety caused the baby's crying. Another possible explanation is that the baby's crying causes the mother's anxiety. Perhaps one way to test which explanation is correct would be to take a sample of babies who were assumed to have 'colic', and to see if they cried less when looked after by someone who was calm and serene. One could in principle get additional evidence by taking a sample of quiet babies and seeing if their crying increased when they were looked after by someone who was anxious and nervous, but perhaps it would be ethically less acceptable to do this.

7 *Comparisons:* No comparisons are made in the passage.

8 *Legitimate conclusions:* No firm conclusions can be drawn from the passage.

9 *Parallel reasoning:* Perhaps you noticed that the reasoning relied on the assumption that because X and Y occur together, X causes Y. You can probably think of an example which shows that this conclusion does not necessarily follow.

10 *General principles:* The passage does not use any general principles.

11 *Flawed reasoning:* The chief weakness of the reasoning is that no evidence is offered as to why the explanations upon which the conclusion relies are the correct explanations. Perhaps the author knows that there is good evidence for such a view, but it is not presented in this passage.

Passage 8

1 *Conclusion and reasons:* This passage is trying to convince us of two things, that crime is likely to decrease, and that this decrease in crime will have disadvantages as well as benefits. It presents reasoning for two separate conclusions:

> It is perfectly possible – indeed highly probable – that in Britain crime is now about to start a long period of decline.

and

> There will be costs to falling crime.

You cannot complain in this example that the reasons are difficult to find, since the passage explicitly tells you that there are five reasons for the first conclusion, and obligingly sets them out labelled 'The first', 'Next', 'Third.' 'Fourth' and 'Finally.' These reasons are summarized below:

(a) The number of crimes committed by the age group responsible for most crime (young men) is likely to decrease.
(b) It is possible that unemployment, which has some association with crime, will decrease overall, and it ought to fall amongst the young.
(c) Effective technological aids to crime detection are being developed.
(d) Policing is becoming more effective.
(e) Social attitudes are hardening against criminals – people are becoming more organized against crime.

There is a sixth point:

(f) Taken together, the five factors cutting crime ought to have greater impact than each would have individually.

Reason (a) is given support by figures showing that the number of men in the age group 20–24 in the UK fell from 2.4 million in 1986 to less than 2.3 million in 1991, and was predicted to fall to 1.9 million by 1996, and slightly above 1.8 million by 2001.

We are not given much to support the claim in reason (b) that unemployment will decrease overall – merely that, looked at from a historical viewpoint, the high unemployment rates of the Eighties are unusual. In order to support the claim that unemployment amongst the young will fall, the passage relies on the idea that lower numbers of people in the age group 20–24 will reduce unemployment for that group.

Reason (c) is supported by examples of the use of video cameras in Airdrie and Bournemouth, which are claimed to have resulted in a drop in crime. Other technologies which could help further are mentioned – a national DNA register, car immobilizers and the etching of photos on credit cards.

Nothing much is offered in support of reason (d), beyond the observation that the writer's colleagues who report on sport say that policing at football matches has improved.

The only support offered for reason (e) is the mention of neighbourhood watch schemes, and better co-operation between the police and the public.

Reason (f) is supported by the observation that as crime decreases, police and public become more confident, detection rates rise and crime becomes an unattractive proposition.

Now let us consider support for second conclusion – that there will be costs to falling crime. The reasons offered are:

- The changes will involve some restriction of individual liberties – we will have to become used to being watched as we shop, or simply walk up the street.
- Society may become more censorious – more hostile to people who do not conform to what other people regard as normal and proper.

2 *Assumptions:* What assumptions underlie the reasoning? First, assumptions relating to the first conclusion. There is an assumption – an additional reason – which must be added to reason (a) – that there will probably be no increase in crimes committed by groups other than young men.

It is not immediately clear what assumption goes along with that part of reason (b) which says that 'the demographic change ought to reduce unemployment among the young', because we need to clarify what is meant here by a reduction of unemployment amongst the young. Does it mean that the percentage of under-24s who are unemployed will fall? Or does it mean simply that because the total number of under-24s will be lower, the total number of unemployed under-24s will be lower? If it meant the latter, then it would not be adding to the point made by reason (a), so presumably it means that the percentage of under-24s who are unemployed will fall. This depends on an assumption that the number of jobs for people in this age group will remain roughly the same, or may increase.

In reason (c), it is assumed that the installation of video cameras in Airdrie and Bournemouth *caused* the reduction in crime. Reason (e) assumes that neighbourhood watch schemes can contribute to a reduction in crime.

We need to clarify what is meant in reason (f) by saying that the five factors 'ought to have greater impact than each would have individually.' Presumably it doesn't just mean that five (or four, or three, or two) factors will have more impact than one. That would be so obvious as to be hardly worth saying. So what is meant here is that these factors reinforce each other, so that each one of them has greater impact than it would have alone.

There is also an assumption connected with the two reasons for the second conclusion – that being 'watched' by video cameras, and living in a more censorious society are 'costs.'

3 *Assessing reasons/assumptions:* Let us consider first the truth of reasons relating to the first conclusion. The truth of reason (a) depends on the accuracy of the figures quoted, which could be checked from official sources.

The assumption connected with reason (a) – that there will probably be no increase in crimes committed by groups other than young men – is reasonable if figures generally show that other groups have a fairly low crime rate which has not been rising over recent years.

In relation to reason (b), we might first question whether unemployment rates make a difference to crime. This claim would be reinforced to some extent if figures show that when unemployment rises, so does crime, and that when unemployment falls, so does crime (though this would not necessarily show that there was a causal connection). The remarks made in the passage about unemployment giving a greater amount of time in which to commit crimes give some support to the claim.

The truth of the claim that unemployment could fall is questionable. Perhaps the high unemployment of the 1980s was due to some extent to modern technology reducing the number of workers needed. If so, there is no reason to think that the high unemployment rates in the 1980s, though unusual in relation to the past, will be unusual in the future. The assumption connected with reason (b) – that the number of jobs for people in the under-24 age group will not decrease – is likely to be true, provided there is no overall *increase* in unemployment.

It seems reasonable to accept that reason (c) is true, which involves accepting that video cameras deter people from committing crimes, and also improve detection rates.

Reason (d) is difficult to evaluate. Perhaps it is true that police performance is improving. It is not clear whether the author is claiming that the police are now preventing more crimes, or that they are detecting and solving more crimes, and thus bringing more criminals to justice. The example used in connection with this relates to crime prevention – the improved behaviour of football fans because of improvements in policing. Perhaps police figures could give some indication as to whether it is true that more crimes are being solved. It is clear that the author thinks that solving more crimes could eventually lead to a reduction in crimes committed, since he says that when detection rates rise, 'crime simply becomes an unattractive proposition.'

To evaluate reason (e), we would need to look for figures which indicate an increase in the numbers of neighbourhood watch schemes. To evaluate the assumption that neighbourhood watch schemes can help to reduce crime, we would need to look at crime figures in comparable areas, some of which have, and some of which do not have, neighbourhood watch schemes; or compare crime rates in one area before the neighbourhood watch scheme was set up with crime rates after it was set up.

Reason (f), and its related assumption, that the five factors reinforce each other is also difficult to evaluate, though it does seem reasonable to claim that if crime comes down as a result of demographic changes, the police will be better able to deal with such crime as there is, and that improvements in detection rates will have a further impact on the amount of crime committed.

Now we must consider the truth of the reasons relating to the second conclusion. The first reason is acceptable. If surveillance cameras are to be used widely in order to deter and catch criminals, then we shall all have to get used to being observed.

The truth of the second reason is less clear. It is not obvious that a greater hostility to crime, and greater organization against it by the public will produce a society which is 'more hostile to people who do not conform to what other people regard as normal and proper.' It depends upon whether a clear distinction can be made between crime and non-conforming behaviour.

The truth of the assumption that these developments would be 'costs' is also dubious. No doubt it is true that if people who did not break the law, but merely had unusual lifestyles, were to suffer greater hostility, this would be a 'cost.' But we have challenged the truth of this reason. As for the other reason, it is not obvious that greater surveillance of, for example, shopping areas would be regarded as a cost by the majority of law-abiding citizens.

4 *Authorities cited*: No authorities are mentioned in the passage.

5 *Further evidence*: Additional evidence might be sought concerning the causes of unemployment and the causes of crime. If it were found that the current high rates of unemployment are due to technology making workers redundant, then this would weaken the claim that unemployment is likely to fall – or, at least, that it is likely to fall without government intervention.

The passage says little about what causes crime – beyond the comments about the relationship between unemployment and crime. If it were found that the increase in crime was caused by factors still operating in our society (the author does mention a possible link between drugs and crime), then crime could continue to increase, or remain at its present high level, despite the factors listed in the passage which, it is claimed, will lead to a decrease in crime.

Since this piece was written, a video has been released which is taken from closed-circuit television footage. It shows members of the public, who were unaware they were being filmed, in situations which they could find embarrassing to have publicly shown. This strengthens the claim that there is some danger to the liberty of individuals when surveillance methods are used. But perhaps this can be dealt with in the way recommended by some critics of the release of this video – by legislation to ensure that cameras are used only for security purposes, and to make the use of such material for entertainment a criminal offence.

6 *Explanations:* A number of explanations are referred to in the passage:

- that the fall in crime in Airdrie and Bournemouth can be explained by the presence of video cameras deterring criminals,
- that better behaviour at football matches is due to better policing,
- that the fall in crime in Scotland can be attributed to, amongst other things, neighbourhood watch schemes and better co-operation between police and public.

None of these explanations is implausible.

7 *Comparisons:* No comparisons were identified in the text.

8 *Legitimate conclusions:* No firm conclusions can be drawn from the information in the passage.

9 *Parallel reasoning:* No parallel arguments come to mind.

10 *General principles:* The argument does not rely on any general principles.

11 *Flawed reasoning:* The passage presents quite a strong case for believing that the factors identified could, in the absence of factors which might counteract their influence, lead to a reduction in crime. The weakest areas relate to unemployment and changes in policing. Even if unemployment is linked to high crime rates, no strong reason is given for believing that unemployment will fall. Perhaps it will not fall without direct government action – contrary to the author's claim that the envisaged reduction in crime has 'nothing to do with politicians'. The remarks about improvements in policing are not given support with concrete evidence.

Negative forces which might counteract the influence of these five factors are mentioned, but the author insists that because the five factors will reinforce each other, it is likely that they will turn round the alarming rise in crime. But perhaps these 'offsetting negative forces' will be stronger than the author thinks. Perhaps those who feel 'even more excluded and alienated' will increase their crime rate. Perhaps drug-related crime will increase.

The passage does not make a very strong case for the claim that our society is likely to 'become less exuberant, less interesting, and in some senses, less free' if crime falls. To some extent the strength of the case depends upon how we interpret the word 'free.' It is true that the greater use of surveillance equipment in the attempt to deter criminals will restrict our liberty in one respect – that in many public areas we will not be free to go about our business unobserved by the police. But if it reduces crime, then perhaps we will be more free in another respect.

Passage 9

1 Conclusion and reasons: This passage seems to be presenting reasoning on both sides of an issue, but does not come to very definite conclusions. It aims to get us to accept two tentative conclusions:

> The statistical evidence for the claim that the disease BSE in cattle is causing human deaths is weak.
>
> We should be cautious about accepting that BSE in cattle cannot cause human deaths.

The reasons offered for the first conclusion (with supporting basic reasons in brackets) are:

(a) If deaths from CJD – the human equivalent of BSE – were to show a steep rise, there would be good reason for public alarm.
(b) Deaths in Britain from CJD were few last year, and no more than those in France and Germany, where BSE is unknown.
(c) The substantial rise in recorded cases of CJD over the last few years is due to increased efforts to detect cases.
(d) Vicars are at greater risk from CJD than are farmers. (The incidence of CJD among farmers is no more than two per million; the incidence among vicars is 11.8 per million.)

The reasons offered for the second conclusion are:

(a) BSE may be able to cross the species line to humans. (It can spread to cats, ostriches, antelopes, pumas and cheetahs – in all cases, it appears, through the use of infected feed in zoos.)
(b) We cannot with absolute certainty rule out the possibility of a very nasty epidemic of CJD in Britain sometime around 2015. (Kuru, a disease similar to CJD, has an incubation period of thirty years.)
(c) BSE among cattle has continued up to seven years after the ban on infected feeds and the slaughter of infected animals.
(d) Reassurances from MAFF are unreliable. (MAFF has presided over a succession of agribusiness disasters, all brought about by its own policies + MAFF is under intense pressure to shore up the beef industry.)
(e) The cause of BSE is not yet known.
(f) A number of 'People Who Know in the medical profession' have given up eating beef.

2 Assumptions: Several assumptions lie behind the first conclusion (that statistical evidence is weak):

- Underlying reason (a) is the assumption that CJD in humans could be caused by the same agent which causes BSE in cows.

- Underlying reason (c) is the assumption that the correct explanation of the rise in recorded cases of CJD is not that there are more cases, but that more of the cases get recorded.
- Additional to reason (d) is the assumption that if BSE could cause CJD in humans, we would expect the risk of CJD to be greater for cattle farmers than for vicars.

The second conclusion (that we should not dismiss the threat to humans from BSE) is supported by an assumption underlying reason (a), that if BSE can spread to cats, ostriches, antelopes, pumas and cheetahs, it can also spread to humans.

3 *Assessing reasons/assumptions:* Most of the basic reasons concern statistics about the incidence of disease, or medical or veterinary facts. Our only means of checking the truth of these reasons is to read the appropriate reports.

4 *Authorities cited:* The passage itself calls the reliability of MAFF into question – on the grounds both that it is inefficient, and that it has a vested interest in making the public believe that it is safe to eat beef. We may not be able to assess its efficiency, but the point about its vested interest seems sound.

The passage relies to some extent on the authority of 'People Who Know in the medical profession' (for example, Sir Bernard Tomlinson). There is no reason to doubt the truthfulness of such people – they do not have a vested interest in making people believe that eating beef is dangerous. However, they may not be in a better position than anyone else to judge whether BSE can cause human deaths, especially if it is true that no-one knows what causes BSE and whether it can cross the species barrier to humans. Moreover, if they see cases of degenerative brain disease in the course of their work, this may make them more worried than they need to be about the possibility that eating beef causes such disease.

5 *Further evidence:* Can we think of any evidence which would strengthen or weaken the conclusions? The passage mentions the sheep disease scrapie, which is similar to BSE and which may have been the initial cause of the BSE outbreak; this disease could be related to the incidence of CJD in humans. It is sometimes pointed out that in Scotland people have been eating mutton pies containing sheep's brains for years, and yet there have still been very few cases of CJD. However, it is possible that there have been more cases than have been officially recorded.

One thing which is not mentioned in the passage is that all three diseases – BSE, CJD and scrapie – can be positively identified in a victim only by examination of the brain after death. So it is possible that there have been deaths from CJD which have been attributed to other causes, without a post-mortem examination taking place. We cannot be certain, then, that the relatively low number of recorded cases of CJD, together with the prevalence of scrapie, weakens the claim that such diseases can cross the species barrier to humans.

Another piece of evidence which is sometimes mentioned is that in some zoo animals, offspring of mothers which have died of BSE have developed the disease, even though they have never eaten infected feed. If, unlike farm animals, these zoo animals have not been exposed to organo-phosphorous treatments, it seems likely that the disease can be passed from a mother to its offspring. This could explain why the disease has continued after the banning of infected feed, and could suggest that the disease will be difficult to eradicate among cattle, but it does nothing to strengthen the claim that the disease can be passed to humans.

6 *Explanations:* We identified the explanation for the increase in recorded cases of CJD – that there are more recorded cases, because a greater effort has been made to identify cases. This is a plausible explanation, but no more plausible than that cases have actually increased in number. It is difficult to see how to settle which of these two is the correct explanation.

7 *Comparisons:* No comparisons were identified in the text.

8 *Legitimate conclusions:* No very firm conclusions can be drawn from the information in the passage.

9 *Parallel reasoning:* No parallel reasoning comes to mind.

10 *General principles:* No general principles can be identified.

11 *Flawed reasoning:* There appears to be some inconsistency in the case for the first conclusion. Reason (a) tells us that if deaths from CJD – the human equivalent of BSE – were to show a steep rise, there would be good reason for public alarm, and reason (c) tells us that there has been a substantial rise in such deaths, but that this is no good reason for alarm, because the explanation for the rise is that more effort is now being made to record cases. However, if the explanation is correct there is no inconsistency. The problem is that it is difficult to know which is the correct explanation.

Another problem with the evidence for the first conclusion is the claim that the risk of CJD for farmers is less than that for vicars, a claim based on figures showing that the incidence of CJD among farmers is no more than two per million, whereas the incidence among vicars is 11.8 per million. If vicars are a very small group relative to farmers, then just a few cases amongst vicars could produce a higher figure per million, even if there were very many more farmers than vicars who actually died from the disease. It is not clear whether the figure of two cases per million applies to cattle farmers or to farmers in general. So we cannot draw the conclusion that being a cattle farmer does not put one at greater risk of getting CJD, unless we know more about the size of these groups.

The passage produces some good reasons for its tentative second conclusion – that we should be cautious about accepting that BSE in cattle cannot cause human deaths – but this is partly because the conclusion is so tentative. If a number of species other than humans can get BSE from eating infected feed, it is possible that if humans eat infected animal products, they can get the human form of BSE; and it is possible, since the BSE epidemic continues, that some animal products eaten by humans are infected with BSE.

What we really would like to know on this issue is whether there are good enough reasons for us to stop eating beef. If CJD is more common amongst cattle farmers than amongst the general population then CJD could be caused by something which cattle farmers *do* which the rest of the population do not do. There is no reason to think that cattle farmers eat more beef or drink more milk than the rest of the population. So perhaps organo-phosphorus is a cause of both BSE and CJD, since cattle farmers are likely to handle organo-phosphorus but the rest of the population are not. However, it is also true that cattle farmers are likely to handle animals infected with BSE, and perhaps CJD can be contracted in this way.

However, even if handling organo-phosphorus or handling infected animals causes CJD, this does not mean that eating animal products infected with BSE could not cause CJD. There is some evidence in the passage that BSE can be caused by infected feed – the description of the outbreak first occurring after feed had become infected, and the claim that zoo animals have contracted the disease from infected feed. Suppose BSE *is* caused by eating infected feed, then if humans eat infected food (such as beef or milk), they could get CJD in this way, assuming that CJD and BSE have the same cause.

There is also some evidence that infected feed may not be the only cause of BSE – that the disease continues to affect cattle despite the ban on infected feed. Unless all the cases now occurring are in animals which ate the infected feed before the ban, then, assuming that the ban has been observed, there must be some other cause or causes of BSE. But if there are other causes, we do not know what they are, and organo-phosphorus may not be one of them. It is possible that continuation of the outbreak is due to the transmission of the disease from cows to their calves.

No evidence is presented that organo-phosphorus is the cause of BSE. Suppose it is, then the general population could be at risk of getting CJD by eating animal products, if organo-phosphorus can get into beef or milk, and if it can cause the disease by passing through the digestive system.

There are clearly a number of questions we would want to ask of scientists here:

- Do BSE and CJD have the same cause?
- If BSE is caused by an infective agent in animal feed, could this infective agent get into the meat or the milk which comes from animals which have BSE?
- If BSE is caused by organo-phosphorus, could organo-phosphorus get into the meat or the milk which comes from animals which have been treated with organo-phosphorus?
- Could ingestion of organo-phosphorus by humans cause degeneration of the brain?

The problem is that scientists have not yet discovered the answers to these questions. So anyone wanting to decide whether it is safe to eat food products from cattle has to base the decision on whether it is wise to expose oneself to a potential but unknown risk of getting a fatal disease.

Bibliography and further reading

Dewey, J. (1909) *How We Think*, London: D.C. Heath & Co.

Fisher, A.E. (1988) *The Logic of Real Arguments*, Cambridge: Cambridge University Press.

Freeman, J.B. (1988) *Thinking Logically*, Englewood Cliffs, New Jersey: Prentice-Hall.

Glaser, E. (1941) *An Experiment in the Development of Critical Thinking*, New York: Teachers College, Columbia University.

Govier, T. (1985) *A Practical Study of Argument*, Belmont, California: Wadsworth Publishing Company.

Norris, S.P. and Ennis, R.H. (1989) *Evaluating Critical Thinking*, Pacific Grove, California: Midwest Publications.

Paul, R. (1990) *Critical Thinking*, Rohnert Park, California: Center for Critical Thinking and Moral Critique, Sonoma State University.

Scriven, M. (1976) *Reasoning*, New York: McGraw-Hill.

Scriven, M. and Fisher, A.E. (1996) *Critical Thinking: defining and assessing it*, Point Reyes, California: Edge Press.

Siegel, H. (1988) *Educating Reason*, New York and London: Routledge.

Swartz, R. and Parks, S. (1992) *Infusing Critical and Creative Thinking into Content Instruction*, Pacific Grove, California: Critical Thinking Press and Software.

Index